Contents

Introduction 5

   Fiction and Nonfiction Share Some Important Elements 6

   The Essential Difference Between Fiction and Nonfiction 6

   A Narrow Definition of Nonfiction Writing 7

   A Promising Approach: Guided Writing 7

   How to Use This Book 7

Chapter 1: Designing a Guided Writing Lesson 9

   Pedagogical Principles: The ABCs of Lesson Design 9

   Development of a Composition 10

   Five Critical Elements of Lesson Design 11

   The Technology Component 13

   Assessment and Evaluation 17

Chapter 2: Letters as Nonfiction Texts 21

   Introducing the Genre With Personal Letters 22

   Functional Letters 31

   Functional Letters Involving Research 38

   Letters and Literature 43

   Standardized Exam Task: The Letter 43

Chapter 3: News Articles as Nonfiction Texts 46

   Introducing the Genre 46

   Identifying the Characteristics of the News Article 49

   Writing a News Article: Junior Reporters 56

   Standardized Exam Task: The News Article 60

Chapter 4: The Essay as Nonfiction Writing 61

   Frames for Thinking and Writing 62

   Introducing the Essay to Students 66

   Personal Essays: The Autobiographical Essay or Memoir 69

   Literary Essays 72

   Persuasive Essays 80

   The Essay on Standardized Exams 88

Chapter 5: Conducting Research: Functional Nonfiction Writing ..:...... 91

   Kinds of Research 92

   Reading Skills for Research 96

   Writing Skills for Research 101

Chapter 6: Real Investigations and Nonfiction Writing 109

   Recording Observations 109

   Interviews and Nonfiction Writing 114

Chapter 7: Writing From Research 118

   Sharing Information Through Alphabet Books 118

   Sharing Information Through the Strip Story 126

   Sharing Information Through Posters 128

   Sharing Information Through Letters 130

   Sharing Information Through the News Article 133

   The Report: A Formal Presentation of Factual Information

      From Student Research 134

Appendix 141

CD Contents 144

Introduction

When I published my book about teaching narrative writing, *Lessons for Guided Writing*, teachers asked if there would be a similar book with lessons on nonfiction writing. It seems this is an area fraught with difficulties for students and teachers both. The problem teachers tell me about over and over is plagiarism, as students write using text sources. This issue of plagiarism did not arise with the advent of the Internet, of course, but it has definitely been amplified by that technology. My cowriter, Kelli Holden, describes the seemingly limitless array of Internet sources as "a double-edged sword," because while it opens doors for students in ways that were once unimaginable, teachers find it impossible to check student work for authenticity. Teachers, however, are not the only ones who find the source texts problematic. Students have troubles too, as my neighbor's son Jeff made clear.

I was having tea with Jeff's mother one day after school when Jeff dropped his books on the table with an air of resignation. In answer to his mother's question about homework, Jeff described his assignment as "dumb, stupid, and boring." (He certainly had *my* attention!) Jeff went on to say that he had to write a report about a squirrel and draw a picture. In the short exchange that followed, he showed his mother the reference book, which, he pointed out, had "a perfectly good article" describing the squirrel (as well as a picture!) and that it was not possible for him to improve upon either. He further explained that he would need to leave good parts out and misspell a few words so he wouldn't be accused of copying from the book. Jeff's mother looked to me for support; since I was a teacher, she imagined, I would be able to show her son the relevance and explain the logic behind this assignment. I can only thank Jeff in retrospect for the discomfort I felt.

Because I'm a teacher of writing, the incident stayed with me, and I have spent years wrestling with the pedagogical response appropriate to the issues raised by Jeff's complaint. I saw clearly in Jeff's response to the assignment that we set kids up for failure when we ask them to "do something" with a polished, sophisticated piece of work that, from their perspective, cannot be improved upon. I saw too that unless we show students other ways to make use of such resources, their only choice is to "dumb it down" so that we will accept it as their own work. And indeed what a pointless endeavor that seems—and is. That was the first important revelation: *We have to let kids share their knowledge from research in formats other than the format in which they find it.*

The longer I taught and the more interested I became in affirming the personal knowledge and experience of my students, the more scope I saw for having students write from the world of their thoughts and experiences. I also saw that kids could conduct real-life investigations of their environment and the people in it without resorting to text sources at all. This shift of focus allowed me to identify a vast landscape of nonfiction writing beyond the research essay and report. I discovered that, in fact, most nonfiction writing is personal in nature, even when it includes factual information. This was, for me, the second important revelation: *We have to let kids write from personal knowledge and experience, observation, and investigation as they learn how to write nonfiction pieces so they are free from the seduction of the published text in front of them.*

Fiction and Nonfiction Share Some Important Elements

The writing of fiction shares many similarities with writing nonfiction, and at least one significant difference. While it is true that fictional writing springs from the imagination, often a great deal of research is needed to support the imaginary framework of the narrative. Lawrence Hill, author of the novel *The Book of Negroes*, cites more than 70 nonfiction titles as sources for his story. Fact is inextricably linked to fiction in countless novels set in real places and in times both historical and contemporary. Even fiction that does not require research to this degree still contains specific detail, whether observed or from the writer's own life, which allows the writing to resonate with readers.

Nonfiction is constructed from the bricks and mortar of facts and public knowledge, but at its best goes beyond the facts and creates perspectives and propositions that allow us to see its subjects in new ways. Nonfiction forms are—or should be—influenced by the imagination and creativity of the writer as she shapes the facts presented in her work. What is included, what is left out, the order and the sequence of the presentation, the slant, the interpretation, and the conclusions all frame the subject of nonfiction writing in a particular way.

It is also true that nonfiction texts, while rooted in the actual/factual—books about historical events, memoirs and biographies, even scientific works—can have lyrical, narrative, and imaginative qualities as well. Much of the same craft demonstrated in these nonfiction books is found in their fictional counterparts, and we might better help our students by focusing on the similarity of skills and techniques for writing fiction and nonfiction, and to introduce students to *all* the genres, leaving them with a solid foundation from which to explore and experiment with writing for a variety of purposes and audiences.

The Essential Difference Between Writing Fiction and Nonfiction

Teaching students to compose, whether in fiction or nonfiction forms, is a complex and messy undertaking. There are similarities and differences between teaching these forms, but the most important difference is in the starting places for each—the source of the material for writing.

Fictional writing begins with ideas, imagination, and an exploration of the writer's experience. It begins with the blank page. And while this certainly presents very real challenges to novice writers and their coaches, it also means that whatever is ultimately produced, however weak and ineffective it may be, belongs to its author. Whatever is produced has the potential, developed through a revision process of feedback and instruction, to be a successful piece of original published work.

Nonfiction writing too often begins with a published piece that belongs to someone other than the student writer, such as the article on the squirrel my young friend Jeff was working from. A piece of polished writing can be even more daunting for novice writers—and more problematic for teachers—than the blank page ever can be!

A Narrow Definition of Nonfiction Writing

Nonfiction writing includes travelogues, committee reports, anecdotal records, logs, diaries, letters, news articles, autobiographies, commentaries, instructions, notes, outlines, summaries, personal narratives, pamphlets, posters, persuasive essays, how-to articles, descriptive documentation, surveys . . . the list goes on.

We impose unnecessary and troubling constraints on ourselves and our students when we embrace too narrow a definition of nonfiction writing. As educators, we have tended to equate nonfiction writing with the writing of reports and essays based on research. Period. There are so many legitimate purposes and products that make use of nonfiction writing apart from research reports and essays, and we would do students a great service by expanding our notion (and our lesson design) to include these.

A Promising Approach: Guided Writing

Guided writing is an approach to teaching writing in which we design lessons that allow students to focus on one stage or one component of the writing at a time.

The approach I have taken is to teach nonfiction writing first "from scratch" using kids' personal knowledge and experience, their real-life investigations and observations, rather than text research as the content. This allows them to focus on how a composition develops—from generating content to shaping the structure to polishing the final product or presentation.

In the beginning, I separate the mechanics of research from sharing found material, so kids can focus on how to read for information and how to master the functional writing skills they need to record information they find in text (and other) sources.

I teach the sharing of information through a host of genres that forces students to transpose the found material into original formats. This legitimizes the many formats for sharing information, provides kids with the skills to create them, and allows students to resist copying.

Once students have these skills and understandings, they can use any of several types of nonfiction writing for planning, recording, and sharing information of a personal or a public nature.

How to Use This Book

This book presents numerous lessons in nonfiction writing that do not require traditional secondary source research. In order to help students circumvent the temptation to copy from established sources when they *do* use these, students write nonfiction compositions first from non-text sources. Following that, students create a variety of unique texts for sharing found information. Students learn to *transpose* information from one format to another. For each genre, teachers provide instruction about the criteria for producing and assessing these texts.

There is a purposeful order to the lessons, which teach students to do the following:

1. Create letters, news articles, and essays from life experience and other non-text sources

2. Read for information and produce functional nonfiction writing to record information

3. Transpose and share found information in novel formats

In this book, I identify the critical elements that support the development of all writing and describe how they work for each different writing task, offering specific and practical suggestions for instruction. I guide you through the stages of creating a variety of formats and compositions with strategies for scaffolding writers throughout the process and supporting them in the revision of their work.

I provide sample lessons to demonstrate these techniques and examples of student work to show the progress they make. Cross-curricular examples show how writing can be integrated into the content areas to both improve writing skill and content comprehension.

In addition, I share how I teach students to access and record information from text sources and, finally, to shape original essays from that material.

Results: What You Can Expect

Following is a list of benefits that I have seen repeatedly with the students I teach using this approach, and that you can expect to see among the students in your classroom.

*   An ability to produce *original* texts for authentic audiences

*   An increased awareness and ability to access information from a variety of sources

*   An increased ability to record and appropriately use *found* information

*   An increased ability to generate and create information through *real investigations*

*   An increased ability to create a variety of nonfiction texts

*   An increased ability to use frameworks for gathering and organizing information

*   An increased awareness of ways to use technology to support every aspect of writing

*   A decreased reliance on copying the work of others

The following lessons can be modified, reduced, or expanded, depending upon the teacher's specific objectives and the students' maturity and skill levels. The essence of the *guided writing* approach is to anticipate the struggles writers may encounter and to build in the scaffolding they will require to be successful at each stage of the writing. As with any teaching suggestion, nothing takes the place of your own pedagogical wisdom and your continual assessment of the learning dynamic within your own classroom.

CHAPTER 1

Designing a Guided Writing Lesson

Since the locus of control for learning resides with students, as teachers we must design learning opportunities that are open and promising so our students are willing to engage in them. If every lesson offers the possibility of meaningful discovery and accomplishment, we will achieve success as teachers.

Pedagogical Principles: The ABCs of Lesson Design

These are the three pedagogical principles on which the lessons in this book are built: every student must enter the learning with dignity, have the support to move to the next place on the learning continuum, and experience success and be celebrated.

Affirm

Every student must be able to enter the learning with dignity. Students have no choice about being present in the learning community where they have been placed. They depend on us to create a space where they can participate with safety and dignity. This means that regardless of their levels of ability, we need to see to it that they can participate in the learning activities we design. I cannot say of any student that he or she doesn't belong in this class. As designer of the learning, I must create a sense of belonging and ensure the participation of every student.

In order to design learning that is relevant, I need to back up from any assumptions I may have about what children know and can do. I need to be inclusive in setting up the learning activities and create choices that anticipate the diverse needs of my students.

Bridge

Every student must have the support to move to the next place on the learning continuum. All students will not achieve the same outcomes, in large part because they do not show up with the same attributes. It is my responsibility to see that each student moves forward from where she is, that she makes progress and experiences growth. For this to happen, again, I need to anticipate what help students will need. I need to design the support and plan the interventions that will make progress possible for them.

Celebrate

Every student must experience success and be celebrated. Ensuring that students experience a measure of success goes back to the beginning of granting students dignity in the learning community. Noticing students' progress and acknowledging their achievement produces the positive effect that is a key component in motivating kids to struggle in the face of the challenges that come with growth. Although the degree of progress and the level of achievement will vary from one student to the next, I make it my responsibility to ensure that every student will experience some success and be recognized for it.

Development of a Composition

Throughout this book, you will see a repetition of the guided writing approach to lesson design, an approach that incorporates the pedagogical principles described above. All successful writing moves through stages in which the writer progressively refines the composition. And although writing is recursive and loops back on itself in its development, there are distinct aspects to the phases of composing as the work evolves.

1. In the first stage, the focus is solely on gathering and generating the *content* for writing.

2. The second stage deals with *form* as the writer shapes the content into a particular format and considers coherence and sensible order.

3. In the last stage, the writer focuses on refinement of word choice, sentence structure, correctness, and presentation.

Students need to be purposefully directed through these stages of the process by their writing teachers. Writers experience a continual shift of orientation between the generative activity of writing (Stages 1 and 2) and the reflective criticism of the editorial stance in Stage 3. For beginning writers, there is only the writing. The teacher represents the reflective criticism, giving the writer feedback and modeling how to look at the work objectively and consider options for revising and editing—what I refer to as the dialogue of revision.

Over the years, if we do our job well, students internalize all that we are teaching them in this dialogue of revision. They learn the criteria for good writing. They progressively assume the editorial role and demonstrate the strategies, skills, and techniques for revising their work successfully and independently.

For this to occur, our teaching must be purposeful. The criteria for good writing must be clearly spelled out. The techniques must be practiced and the strategies employed. And most important of all, students must experience a measure of success and empowerment in the writing community we establish. Although students in any given classroom represent every skill level across the spectrum, writers can be moved forward along the writing continuum if teachers foster a sense of community and incorporate the five critical elements of lesson design into their planning.

Five Critical Elements of Lesson Design

The following five critical elements appear throughout the following chapters in the form of practical suggestions, strategies, and techniques for supplying support to students for a spectrum of nonfiction writing activities.

- Relevance
- Focused instruction
- Scaffolding
- Practice
- Feedback

Relevance

Learning must be relevant for students. Relevance in this sense is a complex concept. It means that I take into account the backgrounds of my students, their skills, their knowledge, their learning styles and preferences. It means that I am sensitive to their particular circumstances, their interests, their confidence, and their general well being. It also means that I understand their need to feel that what we are doing matters, that it is worthwhile.

Any of us who have attended a training session, whether it's to learn a computer program or how to operate a digital camera, knows that it is alienating when the instructor proceeds as if we were much *more* knowledgeable than we are and insulting when she proceeds as if we were much *less* knowledgeable than we are. In either case, we experience the instruction as lacking in relevance to us.

All of us have likewise been in a situation where we chafed at being held captive in a session where we deemed the material useless or profoundly unimportant. While it is certainly true that we will not always be able to convince students that what they are learning is important, we can design learning tasks in such a way that the relevance for them is increased. The choices we make and those we offer our students can significantly influence their sense of the lesson's value and their willingness to enter the learning. This book attempts to present writing tasks that will interest students and help them to see how written language can empower them.

Focused Instruction

Students need to be shown where the lesson is going. Teachers need to clearly show kids what the target is. This means spelling out the criteria for success with every task. For instance, focused instruction allows students to learn what a lead is in a news article and how to use transitions effectively. Mini-lessons focus attention on the how-to at just the right moment. Focused instruction can happen as students are guided to discover information through modeling, shared writing, and direct teaching.

Scaffolding

Scaffolding of various kinds is necessary for all students at some point in the process of writing. It lets students know that you have a net under them, that they can't fail at this activity. Students can be supported in countless ways; sharing the workload with peers, working collaboratively, and working from models are just a few ways students can engage in challenging assignments. Giving students components, such as choices for introductory sentences, bridges that difficult beginning for some students. There are times when we need to scribe for students. Focus questions, sentence stems, and diagrams can provide scaffolding, as can pictures, graphic organizers, checklists, verbal processing, metacognitive strategies, and visualization. This text contains suggestions for scaffolding and interventions at every stage of the writing, from generating ideas to clean-editing the final copy.

Practice

One of the principles of guided writing is breaking down a complex writing assignment into components that can be tackled one at a time, so that we can provide focused instruction around each component. Practice allows students to focus on one task at a time. It enables them to try something in isolation, such as writing a lead, apart from the complex and overwhelming writing project as a whole—for instance, an entire news article. This clear and narrow focus lets them gauge how they are doing and refine their efforts. Practicing a single component builds skill and confidence. Often this practice will take place with the support of peers before students attempt the same task independently. Reluctant writers are more likely to enter the learning when they see the task as doable.

Feedback

Feedback is not something we should reserve for the end of the writing process. Rather, it is essential at every stage of the writing so that students can make revisions that keep the composition on track. Feedback can take many forms, both written and verbal. It can come through teacher comments, well-trained peer editors, or from self-evaluation and reflection checklists.

Good feedback tells the writer how she is doing so far and what needs to be done next. An equally important function of feedback is to celebrate little successes along the way: *That's a great detail, a good transition here, an interesting observation.* These specific positive remarks reinforce the writer's efforts and boost confidence.

Assessment and evaluation rubrics are discussed and presented throughout this book, emphasizing the importance of developing criteria for assignments early in the lesson. The most powerful feedback writers receive is the response from audiences. I offer a number of ideas that enable students to experience feedback from authentic audiences.

The Technology Component

It is my real privilege to have collaborated with Kelli Holden in writing this book. Kelli is a wonderfully talented colleague who has won recognition for her work with technology in the classroom. Her suggestions throughout the book enrich the lessons immeasurably and make me wish I could have been a student in a classroom like hers. Kelli's suggestions are woven throughout the book, sharing how a given lesson might look with the use of technological tools. In the following section, Kelli shares how technology has come to be an integral part of her teaching, benefiting both her instruction and her students' learning.

A Rationale for Incorporating Technology in the Teaching of Writing

I often hear teachers talk about their reasons for not using technology: *I don't know enough about the program. We don't have the latest version. It never works. There isn't a class set.* The list goes on. My own experience is that the tools of technology bring my curriculum to life in a way that nothing else has done. Time after time, as my students use a variety of tools in authentic learning experiences, I see them truly engaged and taking control of their learning. As a teacher using technology tools, I can structure differentiated learning experiences that give students choices and empower them. I can create a level playing field for those who may lack background knowledge and orchestrate their successes. I can engineer the emergence of new leaders in the classroom by creating technology experts from students who have not yet enjoyed special status. This new dynamic adds to the building of community within the classroom. It's hard to think of another tool that can achieve so much.

Our students are growing up in a world of information that is constantly changing and evolving. Technology is used to manipulate information in countless ways, and it is crucial for students to be able to recognize what is reliable. More than ever, our children need the skills to manage information in a variety of formats. As Mary states, "Nonfiction . . . at its best goes beyond the facts themselves and creates perspectives and propositions that allow us to see its subjects in new ways."

The presentation of information has taken on increasing importance in this new world. Visual literacy is, with good reason, the new catchphrase in education circles. Students today are spending their lives online, creating Facebook pages and living in online environments such as Second Life where they are constantly bombarded with images and information. They need to know how to identify critical information, and how to present it in a manner that is educational, engaging, and interactive. They need to be able to make their knowledge stand out from competing texts. They need to be able to use technology to create and share new knowledge.

I've learned from experience that I don't have to be the expert in order to use technology in my classroom; I just have to be willing to take the risk to try something new. This perspective frees me from the impossible task of learning it all, and instead directs my focus on structuring learning experiences that take advantage of and incorporate the skills of my students. Our children arrive in the classroom with skill sets and experiences with technology that sometimes exceed our own, and we can utilize and build upon their skills. I have found that I'm not on my own but have membership in a community of learners who will support *me* in my efforts, and that together we can solve the problems that arise. When we hear about the latest software or equipment, we can experiment with it, learn how to use it, and discover ways to use it to support our learning.

The key is to embed the expectation that students are to *explore* and *discover* as an essential part of each project. This agenda encourages kids to take risks and builds in open-endedness. Each and every time I give an assignment, even those I've done before, the students teach me something new. I know that working independently means that we are each restricted to only our own ideas. Having my students contribute *their* ideas about how to use new tools results in creative ideas and new avenues to explore. Engineering the classroom environment to produce a community of experts means that we all have support. We all have the confidence to try.

Technology can enhance supports for students as they write nonfiction. We can easily access a variety of models of good writing. The tools can provide direct instruction, and enable shared practice. Technology can support scaffolding and intervention. It can assist in providing feedback and provide authentic audiences for student work.

When designing my lessons, several principles guide my decisions as to which technology tools to select and how much technology I will use in a lesson or activity. I ask myself certain questions before designing a project. First of all, is it worth it? Sometimes people jump on the technology bandwagon and decide they are going to do everything with technology. I don't want to find myself in the position of using a technological tool just to be able to say, well, we used technology today. A pencil is an effective technological tool that still has a vital place in the classroom. I need to ask myself, *Does using the technology create learning that isn't possible without it?*

Another point is to consider how using technology supports my curriculum. Teaching my students to use PowerPoint isn't enough. Teaching my students about life in the Middle Ages and having them use PowerPoint as the vehicle for their presentations makes sense, especially since I know that using multimedia (images and sound) will enhance the impact of the information being presented. I have to know how the technology will enhance the learning I am focusing on.

Finally, I must consider how the use of technology will support the building of community in my classroom. Some people fear that using technology in learning environments is, by its nature, isolating—but it can be the glue that holds us together. My focus is always on collaboration rather than having students work in isolation. I need to identify who among my

Lessons for Guided Writing: Nonfiction © 2011 by Mary Sullivan, Scholastic Teaching Resources

students will be my support. Who are the experts in my classroom? Who are the experts waiting to be discovered?

Mary describes three pedagogical principles underlying her teaching: affirm, bridge, and celebrate. I can use technological tools to *affirm* students in our learning community. For some, it will be in broadening their choices and increasing the relevancy of tasks by using interactive Web sites. For others, it might be providing the support of graphic organizers to clarify and organize their ideas before writing. It might be as simple as giving students the choice to use technology in creating the finished product.

Technology can provide the *bridge* needed to move students on from their starting point. Some may require assistance from a software program that reads aloud text from Web sites as they research assigned topics. This type of intervention moves a student forward and takes him or her to the next place on the learning continuum.

I love that using technology can take us beyond the school walls as we *celebrate* learning. Students can easily share their work with a wider audience and with friends and family around the world, using blogs and Web 2.0 sites. We can publish work on sites like VoiceThread, and receive feedback from interested readers around the world. These authentic reactions motivate students to do even more next time.

Are the Tech Tips for You?

I believe that every teacher can strategically use technology to enhance instruction. The Tech Tips are for you if you want to do the following:

- Incorporate more technology in your teaching, but are hesitant because you lack mastery of the skills
- Experiment with and explore technology beyond your current comfort zone
- Discover innovative ideas to add to your technological repertoire to support student writing

How Will the Tech Tips Support Teachers of Nonfiction Writing?

This book will describe multiple entry points for integrating technology into instruction. Whether your experience with technology is limited or extensive, you'll find easy-to-use ideas and suggestions. Whether you have limited equipment and hardware or are surrounded by computers and interactive whiteboards, you'll find activities to try. The projects can be scaled up or down to suit your needs.

Here's what the Tech Tips include:

- Easy-to-use suggestions for incorporating technology to support projects
- Ideas for fostering expertise and creating technology leaders among staff and students in a variety of projects
- Tips on how to avoid pitfalls
- Actual examples of projects using technology

- Models for teaching presentation software and graphic organizers
- Tips to support your own development in technical skills, as well as to support students in gaining more skills
- Web sites to support suggested projects

The Technological Tools

There's no end to the technology tools now available for use in schools, but which to choose? Here are a few of my favorites.

A **visual presenter** (ELMO, SMART Document Camera, for example) is an invaluable tool for sharing examples and establishing criteria. It is the one piece of technology I can no longer teach without. Simply place a piece of writing on the base of the presenter, and the image of the text is projected up on a screen for all to see. Not only can everyone see the original piece, but I can also write on the image as we discuss it. I can highlight and specifically identify the characteristics of excellence. I can clearly label the rich details. Visual presenters provide the perfect opportunity for just-in-time teaching—for example, if several students are struggling with organization, I can share selections that illustrate that trait. The exemplars are not limited to student work—placing a book on the base of the presenter ensures that everyone can see the text and illustrations. I can choose brochures, newspapers, flyers . . . the list is endless. My students are accustomed to constantly sharing and assessing their own work and that of their peers with the visual presenter. Such a simple tool truly transforms my teaching.

Graphic organizer programs like Inspiration, SMART Ideas, or Web sites such as Gliffy and Mindmeister are essential tools that assist students with organizing their ideas and information. Graphic organizers simplify the task and help students produce a final piece that is easy to read (unlike many hand-drawn webs/mind maps). All of these programs share an intuitive, easy-to-run format. Inspiration is available for 30-day free trials, and there are free versions of the online programs as well. SMART Ideas is designed to work with SMART Boards, and takes advantage of the interactive whiteboard pens. The purchase of a SMART Board entitles the user to a SMART Ideas license.

My students describe our **interactive whiteboard** (SMART Boards, Prometheans) as a giant computer screen on our wall. The image from the computer screen is projected onto the large electronic whiteboard for all to see. Teachers and students can interact with the board by using their fingers, pens, or other tools. Lessons and activities on the SMART Board are highly engaging and motivating for students. Because it is a computer, I can easily save, print, and share items.

Student Response Systems are individual handheld units that allow students to respond to questions posed by the teacher using an interactive whiteboard. They enable students to work independently on assignments, receive immediate feedback to questions, and provide detailed reports to the teacher.

Our **videoconferencing equipment** brings the world to our classroom! Because it allows two or more locations to hold a meeting via a video link with both video and audio, we can take a virtual field trip to a location in a different time zone to gather notes, or we can pose

Lessons for Guided Writing: Nonfiction © 2011 by Mary Sullivan, Scholastic Teaching Resources

questions to experts in another country. Our students can also become the experts who share the information they've gathered with an authentic audience far, far away.

All of these technology tools can add richness to the writing experience, and a wealth of new learning. Specific teaching sequences for use with graphic organizers and multimedia software programs are presented in the appendix. Brief descriptions of the variety of Web sites mentioned throughout the book are available in the appendix along with the specific URL for each.

Assessment and Evaluation

Assessment is the purposeful observation of how a student performs on a given task. The purpose of that observation is to find the best teaching approach for improving that student's performance. Student success is an important consideration when I am designing learning, and I alter that design based on the feedback I receive from students. Specifically, I consider the following attributes:

- Motivation
- Willingness to risk
- Comprehension
- Increased skill levels and knowledge

I look purposefully at the individual student's response to ascertain where he or she is on the continuum of skills and what intervention/scaffolding he or she needs to make progress along that continuum. The student may require direct instruction, feedback, practice, or some practical supports, such as questions, prompts, checklists, or graphic organizers. As I continually look for cues from learners, I can keep improving instruction and providing support of all kinds to promote their success.

Providing students with criteria for excellence is the first component of success. Ideally, students examine excellent models and determine the criteria themselves; in any event, they need a clear picture of the type of work they'll be doing. Giving students opportunities to practice with support and receive meaningful feedback is the next step. Celebrating progress is the culminating piece in providing students with the sense of empowerment to say *I can*.

Throughout this book, I consistently suggest that it's essential to expose students to the characteristics of the various genres, and that the criteria for excellence in products and performances be spelled out specifically in rubrics and checklists. It's just as essential to our success in fostering learning that we are clear about these aspects of what we are teaching.

Rubrics are one way of setting out your precise expectations for a given assignment. Showing students examples and models provides the "big picture," while rubrics supply the details. Every learning task will be more easily and successfully accomplished by a greater number of students when we provide them with a visible goal and a practical map to attain it. Students who are then evaluated against these same criteria also experience a sense of fairness and a measure of control in approaching the outcomes we set for them.

Creating Rubrics

If you are creating a rubric specifically for a particular assignment (and that is the best kind of rubric because it is so clear and precise), you may want to consider answering the following questions as you describe the best possible performance or product of the type you are evaluating. (*Note: These questions appear as a reproducible planning sheet—Creating a Rubric: Guided Questions—on the CD.*)

Creating a Rubric: Guided Questions

1. What will the **content** include? (*Consider both the type/quality of information and the amount.*)

2. What will characterize the product's **form** or structure? (*Consider order, coherence, accuracy of format conventions for the genre, sophistication of sentence structure.*)

3. How would the level of language and style be described? (*Consider vocabulary, correctness of conventions, and tone.*)

4. What will characterize an exemplary final product/performance? (*Consider the presentation, uniqueness, originality, fine-tuning.*)

Students benefit greatly from participating in the creation of the rubric for an assignment. The first time you involve them in the task, be sure the assignment is limited in scope. Creating a rubric for a title page is a place I often start. You might have students work in small groups, where more active engagement is required of a greater number of students, or you could do it as a whole-class collaboration.

The criteria for the genre of the piece of work must be clear. Ideally, students analyze the anonymous work of previous students, dividing the examples into four categories according to the students' assessment of the relative strength of the pieces. Groups then present their ranking of the pieces and their justification for that ranking. Once all the groups have presented and you have noted their reasons, you have the basis for identifying the separate aspects of the assignment the students deem important. (Of course, you can guide the discussion to reflect your priorities!) These aspects become the category labels for the rubric.

For the title page rubric, the categories are quite limited and depend entirely upon the non-negotiable requirements you set with the students. If you require students to include graphics that hint at material in the report, that then becomes a category. If you require certain specific information on the title page, such as student name, date, grade, and/or subject, these also constitute a category. If you want students to demonstrate a particular technological skill (e.g., use of borders), that would also be a category. Finally, using conventions correctly and overall neatness of the presentation are standard elements.

Now ask the groups to create a rubric for the assignment based on the categories

---

FORM 1
Reproducible on CD

Creating a Rubric: Guided Questions

Assignment _____

1. What will the *content* include?
   (Consider both the type/quality of information and the amount.)

2. What will characterize the product's *form* or structure?
   (Consider order, coherence, accuracy of format conventions for the genre, sophistication of sentence structure.)

3. How would the level of *language and style* be described?
   (Consider vocabulary, correctness of conventions, and tone.)

4. What will characterize an exemplary final product/performance?
   (Consider the presentation, uniqueness, originality, fine-tuning.)

Lessons for Guided Writing: Nonfiction © 2011 by Mary Sullivan, Scholastic Teaching Resources   **Form 1** determined in the whole-class discussion. For each category, ask students to imagine what an excellent response to the assignment would be. Use these sentence stems to prompt student thinking:

- A great project/product would **be** . . .
- A great project would **have** . . .
- A great project would **include** . . .

Next, ask students to consider a project at the opposite end of the spectrum. What will characterize the worst example of the project? (They tend to enjoy this!)

After they have written descriptors that are more or less the opposite of the descriptors for an excellent project, ask them to describe products that fall between the extremes. This task always proves the most difficult and usually will require your help. Supply students with a set of descriptors such as those in the chart below and ask them to describe products according to three or four rankings based on their work together.

For some simple tasks, or at lower grade levels, you may wish to create only three levels of performance: Excellent/Satisfactory/Needs Improvement. With more complex tasks, more sophisticated writers, or because of your school's reporting criteria, you may have reason to create four or even five levels of performance. None of these are in themselves "the best" method. The really important aspect of a rubric is that it *spells out the precise criteria* for achieving success in the particular task, product, or performance. When we do that well, students understand what a number between 1–5 means, where 5 is excellent and 1 is poor.

You can use Create a Rubric: A Guide for Students, Form 2 on the CD, to guide students through this process. You'll find blank rubric templates on Forms 3–4 on the CD.

Descriptors for Various Levels of Performance

At the highest level of competence:	At the second level of competence:	At the third level of competence:	At the lowest level of competence:
many, strong, clear, always, evident, thoughtful, excellent, superior, articulate, sophisticated unique, consistently, most, insightful, predictably well-developed, purposeful, complete, independently, original	competent, satisfactory, good, usually, often, at times, adequate, suitable, appropriate, shows evidence of, acceptable, willingly, focused	only with assistance, incomplete, unclear, undeveloped, irrelevant, with assistance, seldom, inconsistent, imprecise, fair, disorganized, has limited skill with, lacking in, inaccurate	unclear, weak, lacking in, shows little evidence of, shows little knowledge of, incomplete, muddled, disjointed, even with assistance, unsatisfactory, has limited skill with, unfocused, poor, messy, unfinished

My aim is not to have to describe any student's performance with qualifiers only from the lowest level. What I really want is to give students such a clear understanding of the task and enough scaffolding throughout the process that no student's works ends up meriting only the last category of descriptors.

If students do produce work at the lowest competence level, it's an indication to me that the learning situation is in need of modifications. As teachers we aren't, of course, responsible for the particular levels of individual student performance, but we are responsible for moving students forward along the learning continuum.

Once students are familiar with the process of developing rubrics, it is relatively simple and quick to create them for the assignments you're working on.

TECH TIP

A visual presenter can support the process of creating collaborative rubrics so that all students can clearly see the examples discussed. Once the categories have been decided, you can create either a Word or Excel document with the same number of columns. We usually begin with highest ranking and record their ideas in the first column. For example, if determining criteria for a multimedia project, we might decide on "excellent contrast between font and background." Once it's filled, we have a starting point for comparison with the next column. Students consider the first point to determine the next statement. Using the previous example, they might insert "good contrast between font and background but sometimes difficult to make out text." Students can type a rubric statement into a specific cell, or write their statement with the whiteboard pen, click the Insert Text button, and have their comments changed to font. I save the completed rubric and print a copy. Since everyone has been involved in creating the rubric, there are no surprises when it comes time for the final evaluation. Remember that there are online rubric generators, such as Rubistar (see the appendix for more information), which can provide examples and starting points for listing criteria.

The most important message in this chapter is that there is a critical teaching space between *assigning* and *grading*—a space that allows us to walk students through the task ahead, to show them the finished product, and to support them through the steps and stages of constructing a composition. In this space we try to take the mystery out of how a piece of writing develops. With the foregoing elements in mind (the notions of *relevance*, *focused instruction*, *scaffolding*, *practice* and *feedback*), we move into the next chapter: the writing of nonfiction in the form of letters.

CHAPTER 2

Letters as Nonfiction Texts

Letters still have their place in this electronic age. A former politician speaking in a recent radio interview said that the audience might be surprised to hear that a mailed letter is one of the most effective ways to get the attention of members of government. We probably know from experience that a letter is treasured in a different way than an e-mail. It's also true that a letter is *composed* in a different way than an e-mail is. Because electronic mail can be more of a casual back-and-forth conversation than mail through the post, e-mail might have more in common with talk than with writing. Writing a letter puts us in the mode of creating a formal and, perhaps in some sense, lasting composition.

Letter-writing can be a means to share personal information and information derived from student research. Letters can also be written as part of the research process, as a way to request information. In language arts, letters can be written as responses to literature, or they can serve functional and personal agendas. Finally, letters can be vehicles for sharing researched material through invented historical voices, such as the letters home from a colonist. Composing any of these letters requires students to shape and organize ideas and information with coherence and order. We will look at examples of all of these so that you can design various assignments around letter-writing with or without curriculum-content objectives.

Letters are an excellent form of nonfiction writing for several reasons. They have relevance for students because they are interactive texts that have a particular audience and a clearly defined purpose. The writer can expect a response and may learn what effect his or her words have had on others. The following suggestions for letter-writing lessons require little or no research.

Composing letters that require little or no actual research gives students practice generating material for nonfiction writing, shaping and organizing material in an essay-type format, and addressing a very particular purpose and audience. The practice of preparing informational prose can be undertaken without using instructional time for doing research and without introducing the dreaded plagiarism issue. There are several types of personal letters that afford students such practice in advance of (and separate from) the research essay itself. The following lesson outlines the critical aspects of instruction that support students in successful letter-writing. You can use the same approach to coach students through the process of writing one or more of the additional types of personal letters suggested in this chapter.

Thanksgiving Letters

One of the most successful assignments I have given students was the writing of Thanksgiving letters. Students chose to write to persons close to them for whom they felt gratitude or particular admiration. Many students chose a family member, a parent, an older sibling, or a grandparent. Some students chose a coach or a teacher. We wrote and mailed the letters ahead of the Thanksgiving weekend so they would be received just before that date.

Relevance

To interest students in this activity I shared some stories with them about the effect that the letters of previous students had on the recipients. I shared with them a couple of letters that I received from kids and colleagues over the years and the impact those letters had on me. I have a letter that was written to me when I was 9. I had visited a convalescent ward of polio patients to perform in a short program at Christmas that year, and a nurse had written to me to thank me and to say how much it meant to the patients for the performers to come to the nursing home. I remember receiving that letter in the mail, and I still have it. I brought it to read to the class.

I also told them about letters I wrote as a principal to my staff members. One teacher put her Christmas letter from me on the door of the fridge every year. She told me that when her elderly parents visited at Christmas, her father cried as he read the letter that praised his daughter's exceptional dedication as a teacher. Another staff member told me that throughout a particularly difficult year of family crisis he would, from time to time, reread the letter I had written to him, reminding himself that the work he did was valuable and the contributions he made were important. I talked to students about how, despite the fact that *they* know how they feel about the people who matter the most to them, sometimes it is really meaningful and important for those people to actually hear it. A letter lets the recipient hold onto those sentiments long past the time they are expressed.

I let students know that the assignment is open enough for them to choose any person in their life to whom they might wish to write. I even had one student who chose to write to her father who had died the previous year. The mother talked to me some time later to say how important the act of writing that letter was for the girl in dealing with her loss. I reassure students that I will give them all the help they need to write the letters and that we will progress through steps to support them at every stage of the process.

Scaffolding

I invite students to share their choices of letter recipients as a way to broaden other students' ideas about whom they might choose. It is often during this kind of sharing that students perceive new possibilities. This sharing within the community of writers makes the whole context richer than it would be if writers were communicating solely with me.

Focused Instruction

I share the letters of anonymous former students who have allowed me to retain and use copies of their letters. I also read a couple of letters that I have written to praise and thank people over the years. I invite students to bring a letter of thanks or praise that they have received (or a letter received by a parent or sibling) to share with the class. At this time it is important to articulate the characteristics and criteria for excellence. These are the same criteria you will use to build the assessment rubric that students will use to reflect on their work and with which you will evaluate the finished compositions.

> **TECH TIP**
>
> A great way to share these letters is by using a visual presenter. By projecting the sample letters on an interactive whiteboard or screen, all students can see the writing. As I discuss the importance of specific details, I can highlight corresponding examples.

ANALYSIS OF SAMPLES

We look at the sample letters to see what makes them interesting or moving. We discuss the very personal nature of each one, identifying the kind of detail that makes the letter unique. We analyze the beginnings and endings of letters to see ways of starting the letter and ways of summing up. We talk about ways to structure or shape the body of the letter, and we'll come back to this once we have generated some of the rough lumber for the writing.

I discuss with students the aspects of content and form as they apply to the particular genre we are studying. In every genre there are specific characteristics and considerations of form that differ from those of other genres. We discuss weighting as a factor in evaluation so that they better understand how marks are arrived at. Some of the following criteria would form part of the rubric you develop with your students at this time.

Using a visual presenter strengthens this process. While discussing each letter, it is easy to highlight significant details, star strong leads and conclusions, and compare various structures. After analyzing a piece, it is easy to save the new version, complete with notes and details for printing and/or future reference. For some students, having a printed copy at their desk to refer to is the support they need to get their piece started. This sample can be kept in a writing folder, available for reference throughout the writing process.

Creating a Rubric: Possible Elements for Thanksgiving Letters

- Uses specific detail and interesting anecdotes to present the admirable qualities of the subject
- Clearly demonstrates why the writer admires/loves/is grateful to the subject
- Has a strong and fitting introduction and conclusion
- Has coherence and a sensible order
- Contains a variety of sentence beginnings and sentence structures
- Is free of errors in grammar, spelling, and punctuation
- Has a clean and attractive final presentation

Scaffolding Through Questions and Prompts

For this assignment I provide students with stems for writing and questions for them to answer that will draw out precise details about the proposed recipient of the letter and the relationship the writer has with him or her. Often when students attempt something like this, they tend to generalize. Having said *You're great and you're always there for me*, they don't know how to proceed any further.

I show students some of the questions and stems that help remind me what I valued about each staff member to whom I was writing.

- What do I see you doing with kids that I think is positive, kind, generous, important?
- What is it about your personality that is so attractive?
- What is it about your character and your values that I admire?
- What is it that you do here in the school that others appreciate?
- What would be missing for us if you were no longer here?
- How do you inspire others to be the best they can be?

Independent Work

Students see that by reflecting in this way about each staff member, I can write a letter that is personal and particular to each person to whom I write. I have students set about having them do something similar as a way to generate the content for their letters. They begin with the form shown at right (which is found on the CD).

Writing is work. I emphasize that fact with students. It's an important attitude to embrace as a writer! No one has the written composition on a shelf in his head just waiting to be dictated. As a general practice I ask students to struggle with doing this prewriting as fully as possible on their own. They can ask for specific help, but they can't read their work to me as they are writing. If every student waits for my approval to continue writing, no one will be progressing with the task. While students fill in the prewriting sheets, I move around the class, sometimes sharing an example from a student's paper and sometimes scribing for a student who is stalled for whatever reason.

I am trying to set them up for success by breaking the process into parts and by giving them what they need at each stage to be independent. Students need to trust themselves to begin the task, and they need to trust me to support them once they have made an honest effort.

Name _____ Date _____

Rough Notes for the Thanksgiving Letters

Thanksgiving Letter Recipient: _____

Directions: Think of the traits and characteristics you admire about this person. Choose three or four and provide "the evidence" that he or she possesses this trait.

He or she is _____ . I know this by/because . . .

He or she is _____ . I know this by/because . . .

He or she is _____ . I know this by/because . . .

Example: My mom is hard working because even after a day's work at the clinic, she cooks supper and does dishes. She helps me with my homework and makes sure my volleyball uniform is clean for tomorrow's practice. She makes my lunch and reads to my little sister.

Describe briefly a special memory or incident involving this person. Include the particulars.
I remember once when . . .

How do you think that this person's influence will affect your life beyond the present time?
When I am grown-up . . .

What in particular about this person makes you feel that you are very fortunate to have him or her in your life? How has he or she changed it for the better?
I'm fortunate to have you as _____ because . . .

Lessons for Guided Writing: Nonfiction © 2011 by Mary Sullivan, Scholastic Teaching Resources

FORM 5
Reproducible on CD

Scaffolding: Shared Responses

Once students have filled in this sheet, they meet with partners to share what they have written. This exchange helps extroverts, who tend to process their thoughts aloud and need to hear themselves say something to know what they think about it. It also helps introverts, who are "in their own heads," to see other ways of generating ideas. Hearing what others have written can remind students of things they had not yet considered but which pertain to their own subject.

Feedback From Teachers and Peers

Depending upon the maturity of students and their understanding of the difference between general and specific material, students could (in pairs or small groups) ask peers to be more specific about a certain aspect of their material that seems very general. ("You say your dad helps you with things; maybe give an example of a couple of things he has helped you with.") If students are not capable of giving this kind of feedback, I simply collect the forms they have filled out.

The feedback I give at this point addresses the amount and specificity of detail (Will it be sufficient to create a one-page letter? Can they be more specific?). I will ask questions to get at this specificity of detail: "How old were you when this happened? What was one of the 'special surprises' your dad made for you? How did the coach show that he cared about sportsmanship?"

Because using mind-mapping software makes it so easy to arrange and rearrange information, this activity is easily completed using Inspiration, SMART Ideas, or any of the online graphic organizers (see the appendix and the Sample Teaching Sequence: Using Graphic Organizers on the CD for more information). Once the basic information is recorded, it could be organized chronologically, with each item sorted into the appropriate place. One click and the outline format appears, ready to be turned into sentences. Once the students show an understanding of chronological order, the original information can be returned to the framework of a list. Physically pulling each item into its new arrangement clearly shows students the differences between the frameworks, and displays the differences in each model.

Once the information is sorted and connected, it is more apparent to students how the material can be shaped into a cohesive whole. It is also obvious which chunks need more detail and which pieces are better left out.

Focused Instruction: Structuring the Piece

The students receive feedback on their initial work and read my comments before we progress to the next stage of writing. We focus now on the organizational shape of the piece. I show students several ways of structuring their material. A simple one is chronological order. A letter might begin with writer's earliest experiences with the subject of the letter and move along sequentially as the relationship unfolded. This might work, for example, with a letter to a coach or a teacher.

> The first day that I even knew who you were was the day of the volleyball tryouts. I remember how nervous I was and how you . . .

> Right from the first school day I knew that I was going to have a great year with you for a teacher . . .

Grouping or categorizing details is another simple organizational framework.

> There are five important ways in which you make my life happier and easier and more fulfilled.

> Your impact on my life falls into three main categories: my family life, my education, and my development as a musician. All that you do and are supports these important aspects of my life.

You are a person who makes contributions in so many ways. You create a home for our family, you care for people in your profession as a nurse, and you do so much as a member of the community.

Students need to look at their material with an eye to structure and shape. They must consider how they can chunk the material they have generated into coherent parts that connect to form a sensible whole. For many students, writing the introduction helps them to do this.

Scaffolding

I give students three or four possible introductions, and I invite students to volunteer other ideas for starting the piece. Writers are welcome to use any of the suggested first lines, to alter them in any way they wish, or to ignore them altogether and create their own beginning. I do the same with conclusions. We also discuss the possibility of using a quotation to begin or end the letter. I copy some beginnings and endings that students have used from one year to the next as well, so I can vary the choices I provide for them.

Possible Introductions to the Letter

Dear _____

- This Thanksgiving I was asked to think about a person I am grateful to have in my life. You came to mind as that person. The first time I met you/heard of you was . . .

- There are people who make my life what it is because of who they are. You are one of those people and I am grateful that you are my . . .

- This Thanksgiving I count you chief among my blessings. There are so many things about you for which I am thankful.

- I'm so glad you are my _____ , and here are some of the many reasons why.

Name _____ Date _____

Possible Introductions and Conclusions to the Thanksgiving Letter

Possible Introductions

This Thanksgiving I was asked to think about a person I am grateful to have in my life. You came to mind as that person. The first time I met you/heard of you was . . .

There are people who make my life what it is by who they are. You are one of those people and I am grateful that you are my . . .

This Thanksgiving I count you chief among my blessings. There are so many things about you for which I am thankful.

I'm so glad you are my _____ , and here are some of the many reasons why.

Additional Ideas

Possible Conclusions

- Thanks for being the _____ you are to me.
- Sometime in the future when I am _____ I'll probably _____ because of you.
- I feel very privileged to have you as a _____ and I hope that _____
- This letter is my way of celebrating you and celebrating my own good luck in having you in my life!

Additional Ideas

FORM 6
Reproducible on CD

Lessons for Guided Writing: Nonfiction © 2011 by Mary Sullivan, Scholastic Teaching Resources **For**

Possible Conclusions

- Thanks for being the _____ you are to me.
- Sometime in the future when I am _____ I'll probably _____ because of you.
- I feel very privileged to have you as a _____ and I hope that _____
- This letter is my way of celebrating you and celebrating my own good luck in having you in my life!

Independent Work

Students attempt to write an entire first draft of the letter now. I keep the original sheet they filled out attached to their later work in case they overlook some good material as they progress from one draft to the next.

Feedback: Teacher Comments on the First Draft

For most students, a revision will be necessary to bring ideas together, to add information, or to include transitions for connecting the parts of the letter. I need to make clear to them how to achieve what's needed. It's not enough to simply state that the letter is disorganized. Since the writer's lack of familiarity with that concept is the reason for the disorganization, I might offer support by numbering sentences as they should appear, or using arrows to show sentence combinations that would improve the flow. Students will rewrite based on this feedback.

TECH TIP

A visual presenter makes it simpler to share these ideas. Wandering the room, I can ask specific students to share their ideas if I feel others may benefit from them. Students just have to lay their page on the base of the visual presenter for all to see and be inspired. Visual presenters have a capture mode that takes a 'snapshot' of the work, which can be inserted into a computer file. Using an interactive white-board makes it simple to create and save a series of these beginning and ending snapshots. The list can be added to from year to year, providing a wide variety of examples for students to work from.

Feedback: Structured Reflection

Before students make a clean copy of their letters, I have them imagine themselves as the recipient of the letter and, using the questions below, evaluate the letter's effectiveness.

- *Is there anything important that has been left unsaid?*

- *Is there any better example I could have used?*

- *Is there a place I could use stronger word choice?*

- *Am I satisfied with the introduction? The conclusion?*

At this point, students should make changes as they see fit or discuss any possible changes with you.

TECH TIP

If students are using word processers to write their drafts, revision and editing can be done on the computer. Using Track Changes in Word allows for revisions and comments to appear while still saving the original text. Seeing both the original and the changes really showcases the editing process. In Word, selecting the Tools menu and then "Track Changes" allows you to maintain the format of the document while adding changes and comments. Each editor (teacher or student) can personalize their comments with a different color, and the author has the final say over which changes to keep.

The Tools menu also has the option of calculating a "readability score." Students can calculate the readability score of their first draft, then edit for more sophisticated word choices. If using Word, select Word Options from the Microsoft Office Button. Then click Proofing and ensure that "Check grammar with spelling" has a check mark. Then check the "Show readability statistics" check box. Now, running a grammar and spell check provides a screen with a number of statistics (word count included). At the bottom of the list is the Flesch-Kincaid reading level (based on US school grade levels). Alternatively, click on the help button and search *readability* then follow the instructions. Seeing the readability score jump several grade levels is a great motivator. It is empowering for students to realize that they are in control of the complexity of their writing.

Without a doubt, a handwritten letter is a powerful document for the recipient. Equally powerful is the sound of the author's voice captured on a recording. Having students create podcasts of their letters enables them to convey a whole range of emotions and nuances. Among the many programs designed for this purpose, Audacity is one of the best: a quick-to-learn and easy-to-use program that can be downloaded free (see the appendix for more information). Now the message is available in two versions—as a lasting artifact in the handwritten letter and through the sound of his or her voice in the recording.

Feedback: Teacher Edits on the Final Draft

Students will do a final revision based on my editing suggestions around spelling, grammar, and punctuation. I correct every error on the student work. Students keep all drafts of all compositions in a writing binder or folder so that they can reflect on whether they are repeating the same errors in grammar and other conventions or, if by paying attention to corrections, they are making progress in their use of conventions.

After making the corrections I have marked, students now write (or print) their letters in their best hand for mailing. With these very personal thoughts being expressed, I think that a handwritten letter is preferable to a typed letter. The handwritten letters also appear longer and in some way more substantial than typewritten versions. They convey the writer's unique identity, just as a particular voice does in a spoken communication.

I even mail the letters that are going to the students' own homes, to acknowledge the formality and importance of the piece of writing and to add to the recipients' surprise.

Feedback: Assessment

Copies of the student letters remain with me for grading. The students have helped to create a rubric from the criteria provided through the instruction and feedback, and I use this to evaluate the letters.

Feedback: Shared Responses

As students continue to write for real purposes, they are increasingly more satisfied by, and more concerned with, the power their words have to interest and influence others and less concerned with the marks they receive. (When my junior high students won prizes and sold their writing, they began to ask about dollars rather than marks, and I wasn't sure if that was a positive advance or not!)

When the students returned to school after the Thanksgiving weekend, they shared stories about the responses to their letters. One very quiet teen whose father was a police officer surprised the class by uncharacteristically volunteering a response. Ken had written to his dad, who was also a very reserved person. The two shared a love of the outdoors and physical pursuits, which Ken had written about. As the boy talked about his father's reaction to the letter, his own face was flushed. "When my dad read my letter he almost bawled," the boy offered with awe in his voice. "My mother DID bawl!" a girl blurted out, removing Ken from the spotlight. "Right in the post office," she continued, "and then she read my letter to the woman in the post office." The kids were truly astonished and delighted to witness the impact their words had on the recipients of the letters.

The Collective Thank-You Letter

Having all your students contribute pieces for a collective thank-you letter allows them to practice making those very specific comments that make a great letter, without the

Lessons for Guided Writing: Nonfiction © 2011 by Mary Sullivan, Scholastic Teaching Resources

responsibility for writing the whole letter. When I compose such a letter, I give students stems or questions and ask them to respond to a certain number of them.

This draws from students very specific and individual impressions and details, which make such interesting reading when pulled together into one letter. It also bypasses the class set of general letters that say, in effect, "Thank you . . . it was great"—up to 30 times over! After a blind musician visited our eighth-grade class to talk about her life as an unsighted person, I asked students to write three things that struck them about the visit. Here are some excerpts we used in the collective thank-you letter:

I was amazed at how you read music by memorizing the Braille print of the left hand music and then the right and putting them together! I play an alto sax and for the first time I think I have it real easy learning a piece compared to the way you do. If I had to play the way you do, I think I would give up. (Dean) Until your visit I never experienced meeting a blind person. I think differently about blind people, and all handicapped people now. (Tom) It amazes me how you manage. Me, I'm healthy and lazy. . . . If a blind person can do so much then so can I. (Pearl) I phoned a blind lady that I know and told her all about what you talked about. Now she is signed up to learn Braille. She thanked me, but it's you she should really thank. (Eddie) It takes great courage to live as you do. (Blair) When you first came in I felt sorry for you. By the time you left I had forgotten you were blind! (Edward) Usually in Guidance class I keep looking at the clock, but when you came I was so engrossed in what you were saying I never even looked at the clock. When I was a little kid I always worried that I would go blind while I was sleeping. I admire you for not giving up and I thank you for sharing. (Daphne) You have a very interesting life and I hope my life will be as good as yours. I have what could be called a handicap too. I am the size of a grade four and I am in grade eight. People always bug me and call me the "little green sprout." (Gerry) If I met a blind person now I could talk with him and be myself. (Sharon)

See Kelli's adaptation of this assignment in the Tech Tip on page 32.

Functional Letters

I remember as a student writing completely nonfunctional letters to imaginary businesses on Bloor Street in Toronto. (I remember thinking that Bloor Street was also fictitious, although I did know that Toronto existed!) I cringe to admit that as a beginning teacher, I also had my students involve themselves in this type of pointless activity. Thankfully, somewhere along the way I realized the importance of relevance in motivating writers, and we began to write real letters and mail them! (How novel!)

I have my students write functional letters to experience the power of writing. I start with a simple functional letter of commendation because this type of letter often brings a pleasant letter of response for students. As a further assignment or at higher grade levels, I have students write letters to effect a change of some kind. The following assignments should involve students in the same steps and stages as with the Thanksgiving letters— a continuous cycle of instruction, collaboration, and feedback as they practice to master the skills of the genre.

An alternative to the group letter is to create a VoiceThread [http://www. voicethread.com]. A VoiceThread is a Web 2.0 tool that allows you to create a conversation using text, video, voice, and more. For example, the aunt of one of my students came into our class and cooked an authentic Peruvian meal as a follow-up to our e-mail conversations with her while she was on a work assignment in Peru. Our students created responses that we would normally have put in a letter. However, her job had her constantly traveling the world, never staying long in any one place. She maintained contact with her family through e-mail and Facebook, so we decided to give her a high-tech version of a thank-you letter.

Knowing that VoiceThreads are easy to use and create, we set up a "VoiceThread station" run by two students. The other members of the class took turns coming over and either typing their responses or reading and recording vocal thank-yous. For those students who were slower with keyboarding, the recording greatly sped up the process. These two students were then able to train others to run the VoiceThread station, and we had lots of help the next time we created a VoiceThread. Our guest had a unique and original thank-you in the VoiceThread that she was able to share with her friends and family. Hearing the student voices had a powerful impact. We were thrilled when she recorded her appreciation of the comments!

At the time we created this VoiceThread, our school community was concerned about placing student photos on the Internet, so I chose to have each student draw a self-portrait. The colorful drawings created a playful effect that we were very satisfied with. Students uploaded these images to the VoiceThread. By clicking on each image, viewers either read a text message or heard an audio recording.

Letters of Commendation

I ask students to think of some product or service that they personally admire, enjoy, or appreciate. It could be a skateboard, a hamburger, a pizza restaurant, or a CD. It must be something they have personal experience with or a product they own. I share with them stories of former students' letters and the responses they received.

Scaffolding Through Collaboration and Shared Writing

Working in pairs and small groups, students discuss possible products and services they might focus on, and they share (perhaps as a whole group) the choices they made. Again, I find that this sharing gets the ideas churning for all kids and gives introverts a slightly longer incubation time to think about what they want to focus on. If a student wants to use another student's idea, I ask him or her to choose a different brand of the product or service. In the end students write to a wide range of people and groups, including fast-food outlets, potato chip manufacturers, cookie companies, video games producers, and electronics dealers, to name a few.

Scaffolding

I provide students with a form to fill in, asking them for some of the following information. (Depending upon the grade level and how extensive I expect the letters to be, I might request more or less information.)

- Name of the product or service
- When they have used it
- A list of *several* characteristics/features of the product that are appealing/useful
- A time and context when they would typically use the product
- Reasons why they appreciate the product
- How the product compares with competitors' products
- Other comments they might wish to make that compliment the manufacturer/provider

TECH TIP

Of course, the Internet makes the choices limitless! If students want to write to a video game producer, for example, but their first choice has already been selected, then doing a search can provide a wide variety of further choices.

Name _____ Date _____

Letters of Commendation: Prompts for Generating Ideas

Name of the product or service: _____

When you have had occasion to use it: _____
_____
_____

A list of three or four characteristics/features of the product that are appealing/useful: _____
_____
_____

Reasons why you appreciate the product: _____
_____
_____

How the product compares with competitors' products: _____
_____
_____

Other comments you wish to make that compliment the manufacturer/provider: _____
_____
_____
_____

Lessons for Guided Writing: Nonfiction © 2011 by Mary Sullivan, Scholastic Teaching Resources

FORM 7
Reproducible on CD

Focused Instruction

After students have filled in the form, I help them gather details for their letters. If I have not already introduced attribute listing (see page 111) to students, I might do so here, to help kids think of the many characteristics of a product that they can comment on. I also remind students of the earlier discussions on introductory sentences, structuring ideas into coherent groups, and sensibly ordering the details. We talk about how to end a letter of this sort.

At this point, we create a rubric for the assignment. It is similar to the one used for the Thanksgiving letters but refers specifically to the content.

Creating a Rubric: Possible Elements for Letters of Commendation

- Includes the product information and product use information from the Prompts for Generating Ideas form
- Clearly demonstrates why the writer admires/loves/is grateful for the product/service
- Provides a vivid description of the attributes of the product
- Has a strong and fitting introduction and conclusion
- Has coherence and a sensible order
- Contains a variety of sentence beginnings and sentence structures
- Is free of errors in grammar, spelling, and punctuation
- Has a clean and attractive final presentation

Feedback

If students are mature and capable enough with these organizational skills to assist one another, they might collaborate to check the order of details on each other's rough drafts and offer suggestions for improvement. If not, students hand the rough drafts in to the teacher for feedback. Depending upon the grade level, this might be one of two or more drafts. On the second draft, the student would address editing the piece for conventions. I prefer to provide students with feedback on one aspect of the writing at a time rather than overwhelming them (and myself) by trying to respond to content, structure, and conventions in one fell swoop. See my *Lessons for Guided Writing* (2008) for more on how to lead writers through the revision process as they develop a piece of writing.

> **TECH TIP**
>
> Finding businesses via the Internet is an easy task. Most products usually have a Web site address on the packaging. Many Web sites have a Contact Us page, where comments and feedback can be cut and pasted in for immediate sending. Remember to consider the effect of receiving an actual letter through the mail service, as opposed to comments on a Web page.

A visual presenter is invaluable during the revision and editing process. Alternatively, capturing the image of the draft, then displaying it in Notebook on the SMART Board is also very effective. When editing student writing on the SMART Board, first display the piece for all to see. You might decide to focus on a certain trait, such as sentence beginnings, and have students select the creative pens to highlight each sentence beginning. This can draw their attention to the use of repetitive sentence beginnings. I like to use the star/dot/happy face stamps to go through and mark evidence of conventions (uppercase titles, quotation marks, and so on). Once we've had a chance to go through the entire piece and have written our comments, it can be saved and printed for the student. The next day, I like to pull it up and compare it to the revised version that the student has finished, showing the effect of the editing.

Using a visual presenter means that students are constantly assessing their own work and that of other students. Students quickly learn to approach their own work with a more critical eye. We also find ourselves discussing how we are inspired by others and the ways we can put our own spin on an idea borrowed from someone else.

Focused Instruction: Letter Format

We then set about locating a mailing address for the companies we will write to. (This is considerably simpler today than it was 20 years ago!) I show the students exactly how to set up the letter format, including their address and the date, with the address of the receiver, the greeting, and the complimentary close. Students write the return address and the recipient's address only on a piece of paper.

Feedback: Peer Editing

With an example on the board or on the overhead projector, students carefully check one another's efforts at writing the addresses correctly. If there are mistakes, they rewrite this portion before writing the entire letter with an incorrect heading. Questions can be directed to the teacher if the group is unsure.

Independent Work

Once the corrections to the heading have all been made, students write the letters in their best printing or cursive and mail them with the school's return address.

Feedback: Shared Responses

We reserve a special corner of the bulletin board to post replies. As the replies come in, the kids share their letters. Over the years, students have received responses to their letters and, in some cases, product vouchers. One student received a voucher for a box of potato chips, another a coupon for some free batteries. Students received vouchers for free hamburgers and two-for-one pizzas. One student, showing her response from the biscuit company that makes Mr. Christie's Tea Biscuits, announced gleefully, "There really is a Mr. Christie!" His signature was on the letter. After receiving these responses to their letters, students eagerly swapped addresses with their classmates and enthusiastically went home to write further (unassigned!) letters.

Feedback: Assessment

Not every assignment needs to be evaluated. Students might use a rubric similar to the one for the Thanksgiving letter to reflect upon or evaluate these letters. Post copies of the student letters on a bulletin board. Ask them to

select two or three favorites and tell why they thought these were especially effective or interesting. This is another way of having them think analytically about the type of composition they are working on and evaluate their work against the criteria.

A Variation: Fan Letters

You may want to offer a variation of the letter of commendation assignment, inviting students to write to an individual they admire. Discussion and brainstorming will help students enlarge upon the possibilities: *a BMX racer, an entertainer, a politician, a doctor, a race car driver, a cyclist, a member of a sports team.*

The option of writing to writers can be a separate language arts letter-writing assignment or it can fit in nicely here for kids who are fans of books.

Focused Instruction

I begin by sharing and discussing fan letters, and then creating a rubric with the class.

Creating a Rubric: Possible Elements for Fan Letters

- Identifies the writer (not by name)
- States the purpose of the letter/the writer's intention
- Shows clearly why the writer admires the recipient of the letter
- Provides evidence of why the writer considers the person's contribution/career important
- Uses vivid descriptions and/or precise vocabulary
- Coherence and a sensible order
- A variety of sentence beginnings and sentence structures
- A strong conclusion
- Lack of errors in grammar, spelling, and punctuation
- A clean and attractive final presentation

TECH TIP

The Internet is a wonderful source for finding individuals—there's someone for everyone! A general search term can be refined to a specific individual. For example, a student who's interested in BMX but isn't familiar with any of the big names in the sport might search "BMX," and find a result for a rider, mechanic, supplier, or designer to follow up on. You never know what you'll find!

Name _____ Date _____

Fan Letters

Fan Letter Recipient _____

Directions: Use the prompts below to generate ideas for your fan letter. Write your responses on a separate sheet of paper.

1. **Introduce yourself.** Here you might describe who you are in the context of your interest in this person; see the examples below.
   - I come from a family that has always followed baseball. My mom's team is . . . My dad played . . .
   - The first baseball game I saw live was . . .
   - I got my first introduction to your music at my cousin's place when . . .

2. **What is the purpose of the letter?** What is it that you admire enough about the person to write this letter? See the examples below.
   - Sometimes I wonder if you have any idea how kids like me . . .
   - Ever since the first time I watched you . . .
   - I have every CD you have made . . .
   - You must have had heroes as you grew up . . .
   - I want you to know how you have inspired me . . .

3. **Why is the person important to you?** See the examples below.
   - Your career is important to me because . . .
   - I am taking guitar lessons and I try to . . .
   - A big part of my life is competitive swimming and your example as an athlete . . .

4. **What response do you expect and/or what further information do you need to include?** See the examples below.
   - I would love to have a picture of you from the Olympics . . .
   - I have sent you my copy of _____ in the hope that you will autograph it for me . . .
   - If ever you come to _____ our school would love to host you . . .
   - Will you be touring in Canada next year? What cities . . .
   - I wonder how you first became interested in . . .
   - What has been your single most important achievement . . .
   - Who influenced you in . . .

Lessons for Guided Writing: Nonfiction © 2011 by Mary Sullivan, Scholastic Teaching Resources

FORM 8
Reproducible on CD

Scaffolding

Next, we discuss how to generate material for a fan letter. This discussion and note-taking phase is of unquestioned support to weak writers or students who simply lack the confidence to begin. Since everyone is writing to a different person, it's perfectly fine for students to incorporate the ideas of others into their work. Indeed this is the very way we learn to expand our repertoire, not only of *writing* but of *thinking*!

I give students a sheet similar to the one shown on page 37 (found on the CD) to help them generate material to include in their letters.

Feedback from Real Audiences

Students are thrilled when their letters elicit responses! A blind third grader who wrote a Braille letter to the prime minister of Canada was surprised when his parents received a call from the PM's office. An appointment was scheduled, and the boy met the prime minister when he came to Edmonton for a meeting. Every year after the visit, the boy received a Braille Christmas card from the prime minister.

Functional Letters Involving Research

Students can conduct research to support and bolster their position in letters written for a specific purpose. Writing these letters allows students to experience the power of their words.

These research-based letters might deal with the study of government, environmental issues, endangered animals, or issues surrounding handicapped persons, to mention only a few possible topics. Students can undertake research into opposing sides of an issue, as well as the historical context and the way the same issues are dealt with in other areas. As students conduct research, they gather information to support their viewpoints and then write letters to the people who have power and make decisions. Close to home, community issues, such as the location of a proposed local arena, might spark a project. As part of a social studies focus on current events, students could choose an issue to investigate and write letters to the editor.

A Sample Project: Advocating for the School-Community Library

We had a school-community library in our school building. When new policy governing community libraries threatened to shut down the community aspect of the library, many voices spoke out against the closure, including the students of a particular fifth-grade class.

The students' letters of support for the library showed their understanding of many aspects of the matter, as well as their passion for reading and love of the library. Some students accessed information about the number of books read by different groups of users, while others talked about their own experiences with the library and its programs. Some

Lessons for Guided Writing: Nonfiction © 2011 by Mary Sullivan, Scholastic Teaching Resources

wrote to the local paper, some to the library board, and some to local politicians. The students' letters brought a unique perspective to the question of the closure. In the end, when the decision was reversed and the library remained open, the students felt empowered by their use of language to effect change. They believed, and they weren't alone, that their letters had made a difference.

Scaffolding: Collaborative Work

As with any writing assignment, students need support in gathering the information they require to compose the letters. As a class we might decide on various groups or individuals we want to write to about an issue, such as in the library campaign letters. Students can often work in small groups to collect the material they need. One group might be investigating the statistics and data regarding the use of our library, another group might be interviewing people who come into the library from the community, while a third group might be doing research into the political aspects of the issue. This division of labor allows students to pursue narrow and specific tasks with peer support when they might otherwise be overwhelmed. It also provides tasks of varying difficulty and allows for differentiation of learning, as well as support for learning.

Of the accomplishments reported in the National Geographic WORLD *project called* Kids Did It!, *many resulted from letters written by young people. Years ago, when a then-10-year-old Florida student named David Roberts wrote to the Florida state legislature and proposed the American alligator as the state's official reptile, the lawmakers ended up following David's suggestion.*

Focused Instruction: Questions and Sentence Stems for Structure

Once students complete the research, we discuss the ways in which the information can be framed for subsequent letters. Students look at these aspects of the letter and we brainstorm possible sentence openers; students are free to choose from these sentence stems or create original sentences when they write their own letters.

Who are you, as the writer of the letter (not by name but by description)?

- *I am a fifth-grade student at Duffield School . . .*
- *I am a member of the community of Duffield . . .*
- *I am the daughter of one of your constituents from . . .*

TECH TIP

When students research particular issues, especially ones that are fresh or topical, text sources can be difficult to come by. Often, the best way to gather information is to go straight to the source. E-mail is a powerful and effective tool. Sometimes the experts in an area are well-known. Other times it may be difficult to identify a person to contact. Universities are a great resource. Sending a help request to a department usually results in several contacts or a suggestion to follow up on. Government representatives, public service employees, candidates and groups/ organizations/associations are also good choices. Some of the best contacts I've made have come from my students. Asking them if they know someone who has some expertise in a particular area gets them personally involved. I find that people are happy to help out young students—I think it is often a welcome break from their regular routine!

I have had success sending e-mails stating that I am a teacher or student looking to find out more about a topic, and asking if the recipient has any ideas about whom I could contact to answer a few questions. I specifically ask no more than four or five questions—that way the recipient doesn't feel overwhelmed. Usually, our expert is happy to provide far more information, and often a series of correspondence ensues. When this happens, students take personal ownership of the issue and become very involved. Of course, it's always exciting to get mail, and students will often come running into the next class, waving their message.

At times I may decide that I need to screen incoming and/or outgoing messages. I might have students compose their messages independently; then I can quickly cut and paste them into my e-mails. Students return messages to me with their names in the Subject bar. With services such as Google, Yahoo, and Hotmail, all students have easy access to e-mail. Most already have their own e-mail addresses and are familiar with sending and receiving e-mail.

Lessons for Guided Writing: Nonfiction © 2011 by Mary Sullivan, Scholastic Teaching Resources

- *I am a six-year member of the Duffield School-Community Library . . .*
- *I am a ten-year-old lover of books . . .*
- *I am an avid reader . . .*

What is your purpose in writing this letter?

- *I am asking you to reconsider . . .*
- *I want to show you the importance of . . .*
- *I want you to know how much . . .*
- *I am counting on you to . . .*

Why is it important (to you or to others)?

- *If the library were to close . . .*
- *All these years people have . . .*
- *Without the resources of the community library . . .*
- *Mrs. Andrews has no way to access . . .*
- *People need to be able to read books . . .*
- *Not everyone can buy the books they . . .*

What response (action or consideration) do you expect/hope for?

- *I hope that you will think about . . .*
- *I hope that you will speak to . . .*
- *Please inform . . .*
- *Please do whatever you can to . . .*
- *When you meet with . . .*
- *I think you should come to our school and . . .*
- *Please share my letter with anyone who might . . .*

Name _____   Date _____

Questions and Sentence Stems for Functional Letters

Who are you as the writer of the letter (not by name but by description)?
- I am a seventh-grade student at Duffield School . . .
- I am a member of the community of Duffield . . .
- I am the daughter of one of your constituents from . . .
- I am a 14-year-old lover of books . . .
- I am an avid reader . . .

What is your purpose in writing this letter?
- I am asking you to reconsider . . .
- I want to show you the importance of . . .
- I want you to know how much . . .
- I am counting on you to . . .

Why is it important (to you or to others)?
- If the library were to close . . .
- All these years people have . . .
- Without the resources of the community library . . .
- Our teacher has no way to access . . .
- People need to be able to read books . . .
- Not everyone can buy the books they . . .

What response (action or consideration) do you expect/hope for?
- I hope that you will think about . . .
- I hope that you will speak to . . .
- Please inform . . .
- Please do whatever you can to . . .
- When you meet with . . .
- I think you should come to our school and . . .
- Please share my letter with anyone who might . . .

What further information might the receiver of your letter require?
- If you wish to contact me/our school/our librarian . . .
- We are having a parent and community meeting at our school on . . .
- My parents also . . .
- You can reply to my letter through the school address . . .

Lessons for Guided Writing: Nonfiction © 2011 by Mary Sullivan, Scholastic Teaching Resources   **Form**

FORM 9
Reproducible on CD

What further information might the recipient of your letter require?

- *If you wish to contact me/our school/our librarian . . .*
- *We are having a parent and community meeting at our school on . . .*
- *My parents also . . .*
- *You can reply to my letter through the school address . . .*

These same headings work for any research-based letter. Students may need to collaborate on stems appropriate to their particular topics before designing the letters. Writing is always recursive rather than linear, and once students get to this point, it may become clear to them that they have to go back to the research phase to gather further material to support some aspect of the letter.

These letters will share criteria with other letters students have written. The questions they have answered (see page 40 and Form 9 on the CD) show the required elements for the assignment and these should be reflected in the rubric you create together.

Creating a Rubric: Possible Elements for Functional Letters

- Background information identifying the writer (not by name but by connection to the topic of the letter)
- Information about the purpose of the letter/the writer's intention
- Pertinent data or facts about the topic
- A clear demonstration of why the writer thinks the topic is an important one
- An articulation of what the writer hopes for from the intended recipient
- Vivid description and/or precise vocabulary
- Coherence and a sensible order

TECH TIP

One year, while studying concepts related to flight, several students were frustrated by the lack of current information available in their text and library books. A quick search on the Internet turned up a local parachute club. We sent off an introductory e-mail and received a reply within an hour. My students sent off another e-mail with some questions and received a detailed reply to each, along with some additional background. They were really excited to share the news of the parachutists' offer to parachute into our school field! This was a great demonstration for the kids of how their written requests could elicit immediate and gratifying results.

Lessons for Guided Writing: Nonfiction © 2011 by Mary Sullivan, Scholastic Teaching Resources

- A variety of sentence beginnings and sentence structures
- Error-free grammar, spelling, and punctuation
- Clean and attractive final presentation
- A strong conclusion

Final Thoughts on Functional Research Letters

These letters have so much value. They allow us to assign research topics that effectively eliminate the issue of plagiarism. They provide opportunities for students to explore and practice writing in this genre, which has many other uses for them beyond the present assignment. In writing them, students come to see that their words have power and can invoke a response.

In a survey I conducted, many students told me that they would rather write an original composition, in any format, dealing with any aspect of a narrative instead of "answering questions on the story." Even though they knew it would be more work, these opportunities to transpose information appealed to students more than the question-response assignments, which they labeled as "pointless."

Letters and Literature

For assignments on short stories and novels, the letter is also an excellent alternative to essays, reports, and character profiles. When students have to take the persona of a character in literature and write a letter from that character's viewpoint, they need to have a good grasp of the story and the characters.

The fictional character can write to another character within the novel or a person outside the story. The letter can deal with things beyond the end of the narrative or within the story, depending upon your teaching agenda. The characters can write to the author about what they wish the author had done with them. They can write to the reader to explain or justify their actions within the story. In assignments like these, students need to know the material well and yet feel there is a creative aspect to what they are writing, rather than that they are being asked to simply state the obvious.

Standardized Exam Task: The Letter

In some states and provinces, students are required to compose a letter as part of the language arts writing exam. Below are the six questions I make sure students learn to address in their letters. Students share the mnemonics they develop for remembering the six elements that must be included. These elements line up with the *Sentence Stems for Structure* in the section on functional letters on page 40.

1. Who are you? *The writer begins by identifying him- or herself as a member of a group that has a stake in the situation being addressed in the letter.*

2. Why are you writing? *What is the purpose of contacting this individual? What do you want*

the receiver to be aware of, better understand, change his or her mind about, undertake in terms of action?

3. What information do you need to provide? *What details (facts, perspectives, history, needs) will supply the background information to clarify the situation and convince the receiver of the letter to comply with your wishes?*

4. What is it you hope for from this particular individual? *What are you asking him or her to do about the situation? What will it look like for this person to respond positively to your request?*

5. What further details does the recipient of your letter need in order to respond to your issue?

6. How can you close your letter in a tactful and respectful way to ensure that your request is favorably received?

We examine together successful letters, analyzing them for the elements above.

TECH TIP

This is a perfect use of the visual presenter/interactive whiteboard team! I capture the example and display it on the whiteboard, then use a different colored highlighter to correspond to each of the six questions. Students identify the portions of the letter that answer each question and highlight with the matching color.

Scaffolding and Independent Practice: The Exam Letter

I use sample tasks to walk students through the construction of the letter. I have students work in pairs, groups, and whole-class sessions so they can practice, as well as give and receive feedback on their efforts, before students attempt one or more letters independently. I remind them to answer the six questions above as they plan and write. You'll find a reproducible version of this task on Form 10 on the CD.

Sample Exam Scenarios

1. You are *a middle-school student* at _____ writing to object to the proposed closure of the community library in your town.

2. You are a *teenager* in _____ town writing in support of a proposal before town council to build a skate park in your community.

3. Cuts are being made to the fine arts budget in the division's schools. You are a *member*

Lessons for Guided Writing: Nonfiction © 2011 by Mary Sullivan, Scholastic Teaching Resources

of the school choir, and you are writing to request that a board member attend the choral celebration to see what talent is being developed through the music programs in the area.

4. Permission for ninth graders to go downtown was suspended before Christmas due to complaints from business and community members about loitering and vandalism. *You are a ninth-grade student*, part of a letter-writing campaign to the school principal, encouraging him to rethink the ban and allow ninth graders to have this privilege restored.

5. You are *a ninth-grade room rep* writing to school administration regarding approval for a fund-raising hot-dog lunch program to support the ninth-grade camping field trip.

6. You are *a student council member* writing to the mayor and town council to request that they supply picnic tables and benches for the green area next to the school.

7. You are *a member of the Lions sports team* who wants to create an athletic award in honor of a former school coach and teacher who has retired after making significant contributions to the school. Your letter to the principal requests her approval to make arrangements for purchasing and presenting such an award.

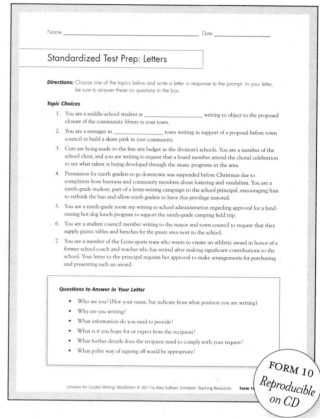

Conclusion

This chapter provides a variety of assignments around the writing of letters. While teachers may find this chapter's lessons present more material than time allows for the practice of a single genre, students would benefit from revisiting this genre over the years, and these tasks could be pursued over a three- or four-year period. These tasks are open-ended, and students will show increased skill and sophistication in their responses as they mature and as they revisit the genres. A nonfiction format less familiar than the letter, but no less important, is the news article. The next chapter focuses on the particular characteristics of this genre.

CHAPTER 3

News Articles as Nonfiction Texts

Most students have very little exposure to news articles. Some current events assignments in junior high social studies require them to read and collect articles, but for the majority of students the news article is an unknown genre. Students need to be introduced to this genre, with all its unique characteristics, techniques, and conventions.

Introducing the Genre

Collecting suitable, interesting, and relevant news articles for students to examine and analyze will provide you with models for beginning the unit. Once you acquire several samples of news articles written by former students, these also serve as good models of the genre and have the benefit of motivating your students, who see from these examples what they too can achieve. The first time around, you will have to rely on articles you have

TECH TIP

Almost every newspaper has an online version. The site Onlinenewspapers.com lists thousands of world newspapers. (The names of various newspapers are interesting in themselves. It is quickly apparent that the *Times* is a popular choice for a name, as is the *Herald*. Some students might find this an appealing topic for research.) There's an endless supply of online newspapers aimed specifically at children, whose articles may better fit your instructional activities. Try searching for "online newspapers for kids" for thousands of results.

collected. I distribute copies of the articles to each student and invite them to analyze the samples using the questions below; a reproducible form is located on the CD.

Allowing students to study the sample articles independently, with a question guide (such as the one shown below), will give introverted learners an initial opportunity to think about the characteristics of the genre. When we place students in groups or pairs at the outset, we overlook the needs of students who want (and need) a chance to gather their thoughts before they share conversation with others. Students who tend to process their thoughts verbally, conversely, need a chance to talk to explore ideas.

To ensure that weaker readers and those who may be anxious about working through the questions independently can enter the task, assure students that this initial assignment will not be graded but is simply to prime the pump for the next activity. Ask students to jot down their responses to the questions about the article. Announce that all students who make a sincere attempt to comply by producing brief notes will have the help of peers to complete the follow-up activity.

Analysis of the News Article

- What is interesting or surprising about the headline of the article compared with the title of a story?

- How does the article begin?

- What questions does the article answer?

- How does the article end?

- What do you notice about the tone and language?

- What is the article's point of view?

- What verb tense is used?

- What do you notice that is absent from the news article that might be found in an editorial or feature piece?

Name _____   Date _____

Analysis of the News Article

Directions: Answer the following questions to analyze the characteristics of a news article.

1. What is interesting or surprising about the headline of the article compared with the title of a story?

2. How does the article begin?

3. What questions does the article answer?

4. How does the article end?

5. What do you notice about the tone and language?

6. What is the article's point of view?

7. What verb tense is used?

8. What do you notice that is absent from the news article that might be found in an editorial or feature piece?

Lessons for Guided Writing: Nonfiction © 2011 by Mary Sullivan, Scholastic Teaching Resources

FORM 11
Reproducible on CD

Scaffolding Through Collaboration

I walk around the class while students reflect and write, noticing students who are not getting started. If they are kids who typically need help or are reluctant writers, I take a moment to speak with them and jot down a couple of their responses on their papers. I do this both to ensure they will "qualify" to join a group for the ensuing discussion and to provide a break from the blank page that confronts them with a message of helplessness.

Students meet in groups to share their perspectives on the questions posed and create a beginning list of characteristics for the genre. You may want to use a jigsaw activity to

An online message board would work well with this activity. These sites allow users to communicate by using virtual sticky notes. Once a student posts a message, others can view and add their own responses to the message board. Wallwisher (http:// www.wallwisher.com) is like an electronic bulletin board covered with these virtual sticky notes. It is easy to create a wall with a few questions. The teacher can create a wall and give the URL to students, who post their virtual stickies just by double-clicking on the wall and typing. This allows students to reflect on the thoughts of others and add to or change their own postings. Introverted learners have an opportunity to process their own thinking and consider others' ideas. For extroverted learners, watching the wall is like having a discussion unfold. It's a highly engaging process.

encourage a higher level of engagement. Divide the questions from the Analysis of a News Article reproducible (Form 11); since there are eight questions, I generally group two questions together, so there are four pairs of questions. Then I create four "expert" groups, each of which is responsible for answering one of the question pairs. Before leaving the "expert group," every member must have agreed upon common answers and written them down. You might add to the questions by asking the groups for evidence, examples, and/or reasons for their responses. (For example: *What verb tense does the writer use? Give three verbs to show the tense. Why do you think the article was written in this tense rather than any other?*)

Each student now joins up with three classmates, one from each of the other groups, and the students take turns tutoring the others in this group by sharing the answers arrived at in the expert group. The jigsaw activity ensures that each student has an answer before he or she is put in the position of having to be the expert.

Extend this collaboration by continuing the previous Wallwisher activity. For students who are reluctant to get started, seeing the virtual sticky notes written by their peers provides inspiration. A new wall could be created with the collaboration questions and each group could be asked to develop common answers and post them on Wallwisher. Since everyone can see all the postings, once students join up with three new classmates, they will each be responsible for sharing the reasoning behind their group posting. An advantage is that students have the opportunity to return to the Wallwisher wall at any time after class. Having time to reflect may generate new thoughts on characteristics to be added.

Focused Instruction: Identifying the Characteristics of the News Article

Unlike the teacher transmission method of instruction, the method described on page 47 requires a high level of student engagement. Next, I want to help students understand how the news article differs from other genres they are familiar with, the story and the essay. The following activities have proven useful in helping students recognize the key differences among these genres.

Focused Instruction: Comparing News Articles, Stories, and Essays

Until I created three pieces of writing that shared the same content but that differed in genre, my students were unclear about the differences among a narrative, an essay, and a news article. (Samples are provided on page 50 and on the CD.) I showed students the pieces on the overhead projector and asked them to identify the unique characteristics of each. I recorded their responses in a chart, which looks similar to the one on page 51. The fact that they had already given some thought to the characteristics of the news article helped them to compare the different pieces.

I find students actively participate in this activity when they have analyzed news articles as a class, which has bolstered their confidence. With younger students, comparing the genres can be an engaging whole-class discussion because of the earlier preparation. Providing older students print copies and assigning the task to pairs or small groups allows them to analyze and discuss the pieces and is an effective way to fully engage them in the task. I ask students to identify at least four or five elements that are different in each of the three pieces.

To make this assignment more appropriate to your students' ages or interest levels, you might substitute the following examples with an excerpt from a familiar story or novel. Create the beginning of a news article and an essay containing the same information. For practice, once mature students have worked with the news article, *they* can try converting a narrative into news article, or the reverse.

> **TECH TIP**
>
> Here's a situation where an interactive whiteboard can simplify your teaching. Projecting two pieces of writing side by side (just create a two-column Word document) makes the comparison of characteristics visible for everyone. Differences can be labeled right on each piece using the toolbar.
>
> Alternatively, each piece can be captured (like taking a snapshot) using a visual presenter, and then displayed side by side on the whiteboard. Similarities and differences can be noted and highlighted right on each piece. Once finished, it can be printed complete with the notations for students—an especially helpful reminder for students who may not recall all the discussion the following day.

Texts for Comparing the Genres of Narrative, News Article, and Essay

FORM 12
Reproducible on CD

NARRATIVE

My day started the way any ordinary weekday was likely to start.

"Brian," my mom called up to me when she had breakfast ready. I groaned and wished it were Saturday, but I rolled out of bed and did the kinds of morning things that mothers insist upon: washed my face, brushed my teeth, found clean socks. I ate breakfast slowly, to put off the inevitable. Finally I was out the door and on the bus.

At school, before classes began, the principal announced that a Brookwood student had won the Japanese essay contest. Some students were making a big deal of it and were all excited. I was more interested in hearing about Troy's new video game, and barely heard the rest of the announcement. What was the big deal anyway? The prize was probably a book or something.

"The winner is from our class," Troy said. "How 'bout that, eh?"

"Well everyone had to write an essay, so it could be anyone," I countered.

"And the winner of the family trip to Japan is Brian McGilvery! Congratulations to Brian and to his teacher, Ms. Nixey," came the end of the announcement.

NEWS ARTICLE

***Pen Pals to Meet in Japan**—Twelve-year-old Brian McGilvery of Brookwood School in Spruce Grove won a trip to Japan in an essay contest. Names of the finalists were released to principals late yesterday. McGilvery was one of 15 Alberta youths who were selected, based on the essays they wrote about the importance of learning about other cultures. Students, accompanied by one of their parents, will be hosted by the families of their Japanese pen pals. McGilvery's teacher, Jennifer Nixey, expressed astonishment and delight. McGilvery himself said he "didn't actually hear the announcement," as he was talking to a friend at the time the principal said his name. McGilvery claims that he thought for a minute he was "in trouble or something." McGilvery's parents have not yet decided which of them will accompany Brian to Japan in July.*

ESSAY

It was in the fall of 2009 when Ms. Nixey first mentioned the Japanese essay contest. No one expressed much interest at first. Students talked about their Halloween plans and the indoor soccer meet, but no one really discussed the contest at recess or at noon that day. Most students had a sense, it seemed, that Japan was a very far-off place, and that it was an equally far-out possibility that it could ultimately have something to do with the sixth-grade students at Brookwood School. It wasn't until Mr. McGilvery mentioned that some managers from his office had just returned from Japan that Brian McGilvery even mentioned the assignment to his father. And by that time the due date was imminent. The essays had to be in by the beginning of the following week.

Lessons for Guided Writing: Nonfiction © 2011 by Mary Sullivan, Scholastic Teaching Resources

Students will find differences as follows.

FORM 13
Reproducible on CD

Characteristics of the Three Genres

Narrative	News Article	Essay
Could be purely fictional	Purely factual	Likely factual
Begins with detail, ends with outcome	Begins with outcome/ends with details	Details supplied throughout
Information leaked one detail at a time	Summarizes who, what, where, and when in the lead	Summarized action rather than suspenseful unfolding
First- or third-person narration	Third person	Third person (could be first person in personal narrative essay)
Often uses dialogue	Neutral language used except in quotations	Dialogue not commonly used
Feelings alluded to	Formal language	Language somewhat formal
Informal language	Avoids opinion or judgment	Often follows a chronological sequence of events
May express judgment or opinion	Headline reveals outcome	May express viewpoint/bias
Suspense and uncertainty create interest	Uses the past tense	Uses past or present tense
Uses the past or present tense		

TECH TIP

While analyzing the three forms, try using a graphic organizer to create a three-circle Venn diagram. Both Inspiration and SMARTer Ideas have templates available. Students can be asked to volunteer a characteristic, then decide on the best placement for it. The results can be saved and printed for future reference. Having a saved file means that the class can come back to it several months down the road.

Venn diagrams are also available with interactive whiteboards. For example, a number of different Venn diagram templates can be accessed in the Notebook Gallery for the SMART Board.

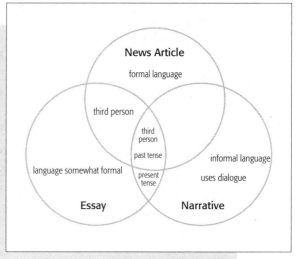

Focused Instruction: Writing the Lead

Now that we have identified the characteristics and noted how this type of writing differs from writing narratives and essays, we look at the "lead" in an article and establish guidelines for writing one.

First, I say that the lead of an article is the beginning—usually the first 25 words—and contains the 4 W's: *Who, What, Where,* and *When.* We look back at our sample articles and identify those four pieces of information in the leads, then we count the number of words it takes to name the four W's.

Then I show students the inverted pyramid that graphically represents the structure of a news article. All the important information is delivered up front in the lead. Information is less and less important as the article continues. This compact format, with its front-end load, allows readers to very quickly scan articles to see what's new without having to invest a great deal of time wading through print to get the gist of the article.

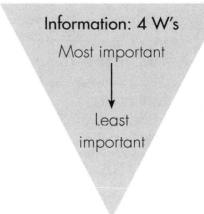

Information: 4 W's

Most important

↓

Least important

TECH TIP

This is a great opportunity to view the articles on a visual presenter, or as captured documents on an interactive whiteboard. Having students come up and use the highlighter tools of different colors for each Who? What? Where? and When? quickly makes this front-end load obvious.

Practice

Before you ask students to research or collect information for a news article, they need a chance to practice writing leads that do not require such fact-finding. This allows them to focus on the structure of the lead itself. I ask students to pick a commonplace, non-newsworthy item or a minor event unlikely to appear in a local paper and create a lead that sounds like the beginning of a real news article. The event can be a household running out of its favorite cereal, a boy falling out of bed, or a girl missing the school bus. It can be real or imaginary, but it must be written as if it is a real event.

We read a few of these aloud or within small groups, checking that everyone has included the 4 W's in the lead. This assignment heightens students' awareness of the genre's format because—even if the content is ordinary—the piece is recognizable as a news article. The novelty of this assignment keeps students interested. When I begin this task with a new class, I share the following examples written by fifth-grade students.

Lessons for Guided Writing: Nonfiction © 2011 by Mary Sullivan, Scholastic Teaching Resources

Newspaper Articles Written by Students

Not Ferret All—Nine-year-old Annie Bohn was bitten yesterday by a ferret brought home by her father. Bohn was treated for minor cuts at the Stony Plain Hospital and released. Roy Bohn, the girl's father, had purchased the ferret to keep down the mouse and gopher population on his ranch in the area. Annie, in an attempt to pet the animal, was bitten on the finger. She says she is determined to make friends with the new member of the household. The ferret was unavailable for comment.

Toe Injury—A Red Deer youth, Trent Taylor, suffered a broken toe Saturday in his uncle's backyard when a cement block fell on his foot. Taylor was spending the weekend with relatives when the incident occurred. The blocks were intended for construction of a sidewalk on the property. Taylor was in considerable pain and doctors fear he will lose the toenail. A transplant is not being considered at this time.

Pencils Disappear—Jane Bollan, a nine-year-old student at Maywood School, has lost five pencils in the space of two days. Bollan complained to the principal on April 10 about the loss of property and an investigation is under way. School authorities say foul play is not being ruled out, but the principal suggested the possibility that the pencils had fallen out of the desk when it was moved by caretaking staff during daily clean-up. FBI and local police continue to give the investigation top priority in the hope of recovering Bollan's property.

Cycling Incident Injures Local Youth—Frankie Alonso, a ten-year-old Winterburn boy, was badly bruised and scratched in a bicycle accident yesterday on Highway 16. Alonso was cycling ahead of his brother when the youngster called to him from behind. Alonso turned his head just as he approached a concrete block on the shoulder of the road. Alonso hit the block and was pitched from his bike into the ditch. The bicycle was damaged in the incident. A passing motorist stopped to help Alonso.

Feedback

These student pieces were edited and revised for sharing, but usually I simply have students read aloud what they have written, and I point out where they are on track and what would need to be revised if it were an actual news article. I might point out that they have used *I* in the article or that they have given us details before the basic facts. They might have included value words like *nice* or used informal language like *a guy*. This opportunity for feedback helps build students' understanding and confidence.

TECH TIP

These sharing times are ideal for using a visual presenter. Using the list of differences or the previously generated Venn diagram as a guide, students can be invited to circle or highlight the features of the news article and make suggestions for improvement.

Focused Instruction: The Tone of the News Article

Next, we examine the tense and tone of these short articles. I point out examples of some of the characteristics we came up with in the comparison exercise with the Brian McGilvery article. News articles are always in the past tense. A writer should only refer to the future if quoting a person. If the writer does not have the name of the person he or she has quoted, the term "an undisclosed source in the Cabinet" or "a bystander commented" is acceptable.

The tone of a news article is formal and impersonal. The vocabulary is sophisticated, and the sentence structure is straightforward. The writer does not use colloquial (slang) expressions or contractions, and the writer avoids making judgments or interpreting the material in the report. Writers use *precise* language whenever possible. (*Many* might be changed to *more than a hundred. A short time later* might be revised as *within hours.*) Experienced writers avoid the very vague word *thing*, for instance. Often students know the formal word for something but use the informal word because it comes to them first.

TECH TIP

Using a specific article on the visual presenter and having students highlight examples help them make connections before writing their own. Again, this shared document could be saved and printed for future reference.

Focused Instruction: The Slant of a News Article

Many different articles can (and are) written about the same event. Before a reporter writes the article, he or she must decide on the "slant" of the particular piece. For example, in the case of a big fire in the city, is this article going to be about the historic building that burned down? Or is it about the firemen who were injured in the blaze? Or is it about the cause of the fire? Knowing the slant of the story allows the writer to decide what the lead (the first 25 words) will be. All three articles may contain much of the same information, but the order and emphasis will be different, depending on the slant of the article.

The first of the following articles seems not to have a particular slant, whereas the second and third articles each have a marked emphasis. An angle, or slant, on a story helps keep a tighter focus for the article.

FORM 15
Reproducible
on CD

Models of News Articles With Different Slants

Help in the Face of Disaster—*There were many people killed and others left homeless when the tsunami hit parts of Thailand and Sri Lanka. Lots of schools raised money for the people in those countries. When a Rosewood student, Amanda Parker, suggested that her school also raise money, the planning began for a fund-raising carnival. Many parents, staff, and students organized the carnival and went to it. $2,500 was raised at the carnival. Parker received a Principal's Award for her caring action, which got the whole thing going.* (no particular slant)

Help From Half a World Away—*Rosewood School showed concern for the victims of the tsunami disaster in Thailand and Sri Lanka. Students, parents, and staff organized and participated in a fundraising carnival involving the whole school on February 11. The $2,500 raised by the Spruce Grove elementary school was contributed to the Red Cross for relief operations in the territory affected by the tsunami. Principal Joyce Owen said the idea came from a sixth-grade student. The student received a special award for her community spirit.* (emphasis on school's generous response)

Elementary Student Receives Humanitarian Award—
Amanda Parker, a sixth-grade student at Rosewood School in Spruce Grove, received an award today at a special assembly called in her honor. Parker received the award for initiating a fund-raising event at her school. Parker's suggestion led to the planning of a carnival that raised $2,500 for tsunami victims in Asia. The money was donated to the Red Cross fund set up to provide relief for survivors of the disaster in Thailand and Sri Lanka. Principal Joyce Owen said she was proud of the student for wanting to help, and for "being a voice for initiating a generous response from the school community." Parker says it taught her that "you can make a difference, even if you're a kid." (emphasis on student award)

Critical Literacy and the Media

This is an excellent opportunity to initiate discussion about subtle biases that the media exercises through what it selects *for coverage. In an article, what is not said can be the result of an intentional focus on some other aspect of the story. The placement of a news item within the newspaper (front page/ back page) or the placement of particular details within the article itself also influences the reader's perception of the relative importance of different aspects of the report. This is important for writers to take into consideration when they are considering the purpose and audience for their work.*

TECH TIP

Having access to online newspapers makes it quick and easy to find examples of articles based on a specific topic but with a different slant. Using these Web sites, it is simple to have students use articles from international papers such as *The New York Times, Moscow Times*, or *The Washington Post*. A group of students could examine articles from different papers focusing on the same issue to provide a strong topic of discussion. For example, the Big Valley Jamboree stage collapse was reported on around the world. The report from Nashville, with quotations from the injured bass player, would have a slightly different feel than the *Edmonton Journal* article, which was concerned with the economic repercussions of canceling the festival.

Scaffolding: Help With Examples of Formal Language

I ask students to go over the lead they have written to revise word choices from everyday language to the more formal synonyms they know. We look at the examples on page 54–55 to explore the effect of the formal language. I might send students hunting through news articles in the classroom for such vocabulary. I also provide some examples on a chart, an overhead, or a print copy for their word horde. I invite them to suggest additional ones to the class and add to the list with the suggestions from other students or from news articles they read.

Following are some examples.

answered	responded		asked	inquired
bought	purchased		called	contacted
came back	returned		came	attended
found	discovered		got	received
helped	supported		jailed	incarcerated
person	victim/recipient/renter/ employee/patient/resident		said	claim
suggested	advised		told	notified/reported
went to	attended/participated in		went	traveled

TECH TIP

Collaborative sites such as Google Docs or PrimaryPad make it easy to compile a list of formal vocabulary and continue adding to it. These Web sites allow multiple users to write, add, and edit writing in real time. And students gain access to the list outside the classroom, so they can refer to it from home or school.

Writing a News Article: Junior Reporters

News articles are aimed at authentic audiences, and this creates motivation for writers. Having students write news articles about activities going on in the classroom or the school is also an excellent way to inform the community of the good things that are happening in your school. The school's PA system, classroom/school newsletter, pride boards, and the local press are all vehicles for publishing student news articles. Students can interview teachers, board members, parents, coaches, and other students to gain the breadth of information needed to write solid news articles about a variety of events and issues. The following is only the beginning of a list of possible topics.

Good news

- Grants awarded to the school for a drama program, music program, playground, computer lab, and so on
- Local student(s) chosen for trip to Ottawa (social studies contest), as Environment Minister for the Day, as ambassador to United Nations Children's Conference on the Environment
- Students receive awards in sports, for artwork, for academics, for performing arts
- Students participate or perform in local events, such as the science fair, the Hi Q tournament, the school play, a Christmas concert, or the book fair
- Results/information on fund-raisers for school trip, activity, or charitable cause
- Teacher wins or is nominated for special award
- Teacher initiates a new program
- D.A.R.E. program
- New teacher joins staff

Unwelcome News

- Shortages of funds or staff; cuts to programs
- Student or staff member hurt
- Vandalism, theft, break-in
- Exchange trip canceled

Scaffolding: Silent Collaboration With Peers

Here's an alternative (or an addition) to class brainstorming as a way to generate writing material: have students provide a brief written suggestion to classmates' topic ideas. Students write the topic of their proposed article in the middle of a piece of paper, which is then passed to five other students. Students receiving the topic write a suggestion, a question, or a comment that might help the writer think of ways to develop the idea or suggest sources he or she might use. This method of quiet collaboration can be very effective. Having students initial their suggestions can discourage silly and inappropriate comments. This pass-around also opens up ideas and possibilities for all participants as they see the suggestions on several different sheets. It asks for their thoughts and suggestions in a nonthreatening environment, and it calls for total participation. Every student is engaged!

> **TECH TIP**
>
> Blogs are rapidly growing in popularity with many classes and schools. They can be considered an online news source and a great place to publish student articles. Any of the articles that are published in the newsletter or local paper could also be posted online. Interested family and friends can easily become part of the audience. A great place to begin with blogging is the Web site Edublog (http://edublogs.org).

Here is a sample of silent collaboration notes.

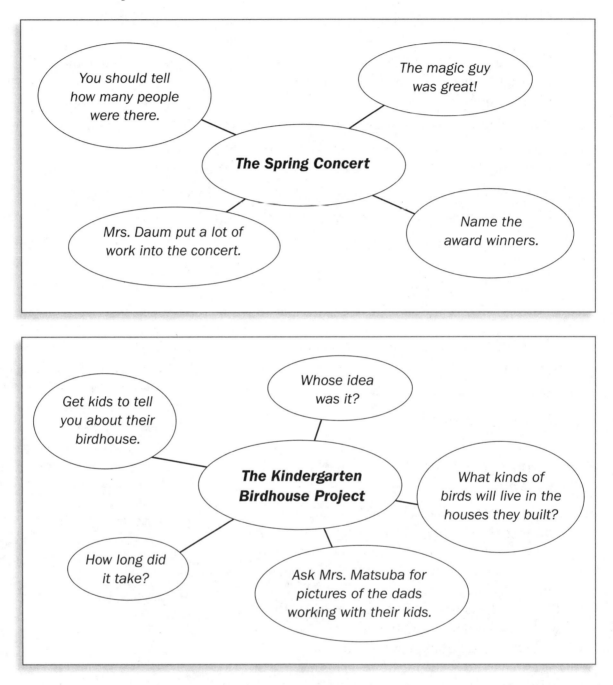

Scaffolding: Support for Structure

When students begin their research for the article, I provide them with a form to give some structure to their approach. (See sample on page 59; a reproducible version of the form can be found on the CD.) They start by filling in what they know. This also helps them see what additional information they may need.

Lessons for Guided Writing: Nonfiction © 2011 by Mary Sullivan, Scholastic Teaching Resources

Feedback

I ask students to hand in their notes so I can quickly see who needs help. If they have everything filled in and I see they're on track, they have permission to go ahead and write a draft of their article. Doing this saves them writing an article that, for one or more reasons, will not be satisfactory. This form is also easy for me to respond to, since I'm looking only for the required components.

Assessment

By now, students have had practice creating rubrics, so making one for the news article should be quite straightforward. The form above will be useful in creating the rubric, as will the list of characteristics of the news article.

Creating a Rubric: Possible Elements for News Articles

- Answers to the 4 W's—Who/What/Where/When—occur in the first 25 to 30 words.

- The lead is concise and to the point

- Formal vocabulary is used throughout

- Past tense is used throughout

- The facts are correct

- Additional information about why and how the event unfolded is provided

- Quotes from persons involved or from bystanders have been included

Name _____ Date _____

Notes for My News Article

Directions: Complete the prompts below to plan for writing your news article. Use additional paper if you need more room.

1. I will write about:

2. I already know the answers to these questions:
   Who?
   What?
   Where?
   When?
   How?
   Why?

3. I also know this additional information:

4. Some thing(s) I need to find out or check:

5. People or places where I might be able to get this information:

6. Possible headline for my story:

7. Possible lead for my story:

FORM 16
Reproducible on CD

Lessons for Guided Writing: Nonfiction © 2011 by Mary Sullivan, Scholastic Teaching Resources   Form

- The headline is effective and fitting for the article's content and slant
- Spelling, punctuation, and grammar are correct

Standardized Exam Task: The News Article

Students are sometimes required to write a news article as a component of standardized writing exams. I make sure that my students are clear on the difference between an article and other formats (especially essays). They learn the elements of the lead (the 4 W's) and practice writing some. The lead is the most important aspect of the news article. If students get that right, they will be at least marginally successful with the task. I teach them to circle verbs and nouns and try to elevate their vocabulary by making formal substitutes for everyday words, as we have practiced doing. I have students check that they have not used the first person and that their piece is free of judgments and interpretations. I remind them that if the prompts give them information about various aspects of an event, they should choose a single aspect (slant) to highlight while subordinating other information toward the end of the article.

Conclusion

While it is important for students to gain familiarity and skill with the writing of a news article, the single genre that will dominate their academic lives is the essay. Feedback from the evaluators of provincial exams at the grade 12 level in Canada one year noted "fuzzy thinking" as a main problem with high school writers. I take this to be, at least in part, evidence that students lack *thinking frameworks* for shaping information into coherent organizational structures. For this reason, I spend a great deal of time and energy trying to show students strategies for organizing the raw material for writing. This aspect is a main focus in the following chapter on essay writing.

CHAPTER 4

The Essay as Nonfiction Writing

Teachers sometimes use the terms *essay* and *report* interchangeably, but the essay, in its many variations (even when it is written to inform), tends to express the writer's viewpoint, opinion, reflections, and/or personal experience. The report, which is more akin to the news article, is a neutral and more strictly factual composition.

Relevance

Because students require essay-writing skills in order to share information for many purposes, we need to teach this format. Personal essays, literary essays, and persuasive essays are all excellent vehicles for teaching students how to generate, shape, and present information. Through these essay formats, students can concentrate on mastering the structural aspects of essay writing free from the influence of another writer's published text. Most students will be required at different points in their academic careers to write essays from scratch on standardized tests. So it makes sense to isolate the skill and guide students through the process of developing an essay.

As students write personal essays, they can draw from their experience to write descriptive, narrative, persuasive, and expository essays. Whether such an essay extols the virtues of the cell phone, describes a skate park, or outlines the dangers of working as a babysitter, it can be a vehicle for learning about the structure of the genre and practicing writing in this format. A benefit of beginning with personal material is that we can hook into subjects that kids are passionate about or at least familiar with, as opposed to topics that are mandated.

Frames for Thinking and Writing

Before we begin any essay-writing assignment, I introduce students to a handful of useful concept frames for thinking and writing. These frames act as metacognitive supports in two important ways: they help students to generate ideas for writing and organize that material into coherent structures. Our most skilled writers may do these things without being directly taught such strategies. They learn these things through observing, listening, and reading in attentive ways. But even these students can gain facility and skill by having the techniques they use articulated.

The way you introduce these frames will vary depending on your students' experience and your teaching goals. You might introduce one frame at time, offering students multiple opportunities to use it before you introduce another. Once students are familiar with several frames, I sometimes have them work in groups to generate ideas about the same topic using different frames, so they get a better sense of how each one works and where each is most effectively used.

Pages 62–65 describe the five frames I teach. The lessons on autobiographical, literary, and persuasive essays that follow demonstrate how the frames support students' understanding of the various compositions.

> *Depending on the assignment, I still use other aids to generate information. I use visualization, attribute listing, stems, and focus questions to help students generate and locate material for writing. These frames are another set of tools for generating ideas when students are required to do that without help.*

Chronology

One of the easiest frameworks to remember and to use is chronology, wherein material is presented sequentially from beginning to end.

Chronology is a simple but effective organizational structure for gathering and sharing information. To use this organizational frame, a writer looks at his or her brainstorming and notes and tries to identify a time sequence that would work to shape the information effectively, such as from beginning to end, morning until night, start to finish, or birth to death.

Some examples of topics organized this way might be the following:

- My introduction to hockey was . . .

- I first heard that my family intended to move to the U.S. when . . .

- The first thing you need to learn about skateboarding is . . .

- All of us use technology from morning until night.

- Right from the moment my parents drove away I knew I wasn't gong to enjoy summer camp.

- The novel starts with the birth of the Grahams' daughter, Amanda.
- Teachers colored my learning journey right from Mrs. Forrester in kindergarten through Mr. Boschman in Physics 30.
- The first stage of the moon is called . . .
- I made my first kite in grade 4 as part of a science project.

With this framework, the writer starts at the beginning and moves through the major points in a sequence from start to finish. Once the writer has chosen this framework, he or she chunks the essay material and sequences it in a sensible order. A graphic organizer for the chronology framework is on Form 17 on the CD.

Opposites

The opposites framework offers a number of options for organizing information in persuasive and comparative essays. I use the terms *compare* and *contrast* when teaching this frame, but *opposites* is actually a broader category within which we can compare and contrast. Kids seem to hang onto *opposites* more easily because it's the word they have associated with this concept since primary school.

In using this frame, the writer looks at his or her brainstorming or rough notes to see if it's possible to structure the piece on opposites: before and after, positive and negative, interior and exterior, things known and unknown, the hero and the villain, the costs and benefits, the strengths and weaknesses, and so on.

The following are examples of topics that might be organized by framing opposites:

- My life before the accident was . . .
- The challenges of having diabetes are many, but some positive experiences have resulted for me . . .
- There are things I loved about the trip and things I have trouble putting behind me.
- Godwin had many strengths and some critical weaknesses.
- There were definitely gains and losses resulting from the years I played hockey.
- In the story, Joy seems a confident teen, but her thoughts and feelings paint a different picture.

This structure generally requires the writer to discuss a number of main ideas regarding each of the two opposing elements. One can go back and forth between the two sides throughout the piece (*Roman is dark and heavyset, whereas David is slender and fair*) or simply give all the details on one side of the ledger and then all the details on the other side (*Roman is dark and heavyset. He broods about things and seldom expresses his feelings. David, on the other hand . . .*). A graphic organizer for the opposites framework is on Form 18 on the CD.

Categories

Categorizing details about a topic can be an organizational framework for writing. It is important when students use this framework that they name the category beyond saying three "things." *Things* allows students to combine ideas which have little or nothing in common. For example, three things about Goldilocks might be that she is a young girl, that she has blond hair, and she goes for walks in the woods. These pieces of information hardly have the potential for a coherent piece of writing. Three characteristics of Goldilocks that lead to the story problem, on the other hand, or three examples of Goldilocks' bad manners, could be the basis for a coherent paragraph. In establishing the category of ideas, a writer is already working toward shaping the material in a sensible way.

Here are examples of how the categories frame can work for a variety of topics:

- Three important personality traits of the novel's main character . . .
- Three time periods covered by the novel . . .
- Three generations of Campbells are presented in the story . . .
- Three important aspects of the care of a pet . . .
- Three reasons why I want to pursue a career as an engineer . . .
- Three benefits of my part-time job . . .
- Three cautions I have for those considering taking up babysitting as a way to make money . . .
- Three ways to quit smoking . . .
- Three reasons for recommending this book to my peers . . .
- Three ways to prepare for a test . . .
- Three areas where anyone can save money . . .
- Three strengths I possess . . .
- Three really annoying habits of my brother . . .
- Three important characteristics of a hero . . .

A graphic organizer for the categories framework is on Form 19 on the CD.

Concentric Circles

FORM 20
Reproducible on CD

Concentric circles is a frame in which the smallest component of the subject (say, the individual) is in a small circle in the center of the page; a slightly larger circle contains a larger unit, such as the family, and the circles continue getting larger as the subjects become larger—the community, the country, and the world, for example. If smoking is the topic, the concentric circles frame would help a writer organize ideas around the effects of smoking on the individual, on his family, on the community, and on the health care of the nation.

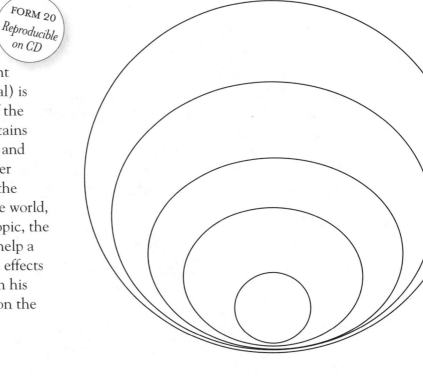

Spokes in a Wheel

FORM 21
Reproducible on CD

The spokes-in-a-wheel frame helps students represent several aspects of a topic. The topic itself—say, school uniforms—appears in the center of the page. Spokes radiate off it, each representing an important aspect of the topic, such as, for our uniform example, freedom of expression, cost, safety, peer pressure. To generate ideas for an essay on the positive aspects of life in my town, I could use the spokes-in-a-wheel frame to think about the services and attractions the town has to offer in all the different areas of life. A graphic organizer for the spokes-in-a-wheel framework is on Form 21 on the CD.

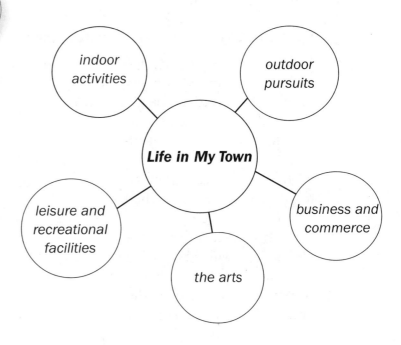

Introducing the Essay to Students

In this next section, I share a lesson on the "big picture" of essay writing, a kind of walk-through of how an essay is built from beginning to end. I also want to show students where the frames for thinking and writing fit into the process.

Some students simply can't attend to the parts (such as choosing a frame) until they understand how the parts fit into the larger process of writing an essay. Other students are overwhelmed by the thought of writing an entire essay and hold their breath until we come back to working on one element, one step at a time. I try to balance instruction to support both kinds of students.

Focused Instruction: Generating Ideas

I often use a shared-writing approach to show students how to generate ideas for writing about a topic. For a number of students, this way of walking them through the process is more helpful and supportive than an explanation. Let's say we are planning to write an essay about the possible negative aspects of babysitting. The first time we brainstorm ideas, we might do it together. I would ask students first to jot down on a piece of paper anything they can think of that would be problematic or unpleasant for a babysitter. (If they have not been one, they might think of their own experiences of having someone babysit them.) I give them a moment to think before they begin sharing. This gives the introverts a chance to collect their thoughts. As they offer suggestions, I note these ideas on a chart, an overhead, or on the board. I point out to students that this is a way of beginning a piece of writing, by simply generating as many ideas as I can without judging any of them.

I often have students brainstorm in pairs or groups of three. They jot things down in silence for one minute and then share what they've written. (Using index cards or sticky notes allows students to group their ideas easily in the next part of the lesson.) I explain, "If you were working alone, you would start this way, by scribbling down everything and anything you could think of that had to do with the topic. It's like building with Legos:

Lessons for Guided Writing: Nonfiction © 2011 by Mary Sullivan, Scholastic Teaching Resources

first you need to dump out all the pieces to see what you have to work with. Various pieces, such as wheels or propellers, will lead you to imagine a different structure than windows and roof pieces will."

Focused Instruction: Organizing Details

Now I want students to see that we need to find some commonalities among the various details so that we can chunk them together into three categories. On the overhead I begin to create sorting bins for ideas. "Some of these details," I point out, "suggest that babysitting can be dangerous. Which details fit there? Other details just show that babysitting is stressful. Which details suggest that? Some of you have indicated that you had misconceptions about the job until you tried it. Let's put those together." We have created three categories of negative aspects of babysitting. We may not have enough examples in each section, so we go back to generating ideas and come up with a few more, because we want to have several examples under each one.

Our introduction will set the direction of the piece, making the assertion that babysitting is an undesirable occupation. Because we are using three chunks of details (the dangers, the stresses, and the illusions people have about the job), the composition will have four or five paragraphs, depending on whether or not the piece ends in the paragraph containing the last "chunk" or has a separate, concluding paragraph.

> TECH TIP
>
> A graphic organizer is ideal for this activity. It is easy to scribble down all kinds of ideas and then, with a few swift clicks, the random assortment of notes transforms into a legible, organized outline. Pen-and-paper mind maps can be frustrating because students have to carefully plan out where each topic will fit and leave enough space for any new ideas. These electronic versions never run out of room and are always neat and colorful.

- **Paragraph 1** of "*Babysitter Beware*":
  Babysitting might seem like a good way to make money if you lack the training or interest in a more formal job. I can tell you, however, from my vast and painful experience that there are cautions to consider before you take this up. The first is, think about your safety. (The babysitting course focuses on the child's safety, but who talks about your safety?!) The second is, consider your sanity! And the third is, lose your illusions!

- **Paragraph 2:** Give examples/details of the dangers to the babysitter.

- **Paragraph 3:** Give examples/details of the mental strain and stress.

- **Paragraph 4:** Highlight some illusions that people who haven't done it might hold about the job.

- **Paragraph 5:** Sum up. Are you still at it (why/how/with what scars?) or, instead, cleaning the penguin house at the zoo?

Practice

Once we have walked through the process together, I have students generate ideas and create organizational structures for the material together and independently. Students can work in groups using the same details on babysitting to create a structure different from the one we made together. They might present the three ways kids can sabotage a babysitter, the three strategies a babysitter can use to protect himself, or the three worst scenarios a babysitter can encounter. They might use a chronological frame to present the negative aspects of babysitting, from beginning of the evening to end.

Students don't need to compose entire essays in order to practice organizing information in a variety of structures. Students can generate material (or be *given* material) to practice structuring using the various frames. In fact, the more opportunities they have to generate and organize ideas, the better prepared they will be to actually write, since these are for most students the two biggest barriers to writing. This practice can be done collaboratively at first to give students support, and then independently, before they write any official essays. I need to be able to give students feedback on short pieces of writing, and students need the luxury of being able to focus solely on the one particular skill I am trying to teach.

Students writing essay-type and long-answer exam questions or taking standardized writing tests should by now have internalized (through instruction and practice) the use of these organizational frameworks. Furthermore they should be instructed and encouraged to choose from these techniques and use them in any circumstances in which they are writing under pressure. (See The Essay on Standardized Exams on page 88.)

> *Guided writing is an approach in which we take things apart for learners. One skill, one component at a time. We model, we instruct, we practice, and we give feedback in continuous loops adding layers of knowledge, skill, and sophistication to fundamental building blocks with which they have experienced success.*

TECH TIP

Working through several examples of frameworks with a graphic organizer provides extensive practice in generating and organizing information in these structures. The first example could be whole-class generated, the next completed in a small group, and finally, independently created mind maps. The ease of using this technology to work through the process to reach the final product can be a relief for some students.

Lessons for Guided Writing: Nonfiction © 2011 by Mary Sullivan, Scholastic Teaching Resources

Personal Essays: The Autobiographical Essay or Memoir

Once I have introduced the process of essay writing, modeled the use of the frames for generating and organizing material, and given students opportunities to work with these concepts, we are ready to write a complete composition. I begin with the personal essay.

Relevance

This assignment focuses on the student's own life and as such can be a worthy and interesting subject for the writer and for the teacher. The choice between the two topics (autobiography or memoir) is a significant aspect of the assignment. Students who deem their lives uninteresting have some choices here. The autobiography can be more or less a chronological inventory, with little private information shared. It can talk about schools attended and childhood illnesses suffered. It could tell how one's name was chosen, or provide a list of siblings. It can reveal as much or as little about the student as the writer chooses. Unlike a memoir, the autobiographical essay has a built-in chronological structure.

The memoir, because it focuses on themes (or even a single theme) in a person's life, allows the writer to expand upon and explore a single aspect of her life while ignoring all the rest of the details an autobiography would include. For instance, a student might write about the way his Asian heritage affects every aspect of his life, from the name he was given to the food he eats. It may open a whole area of culture and language to him that his peers do not share or have any real knowledge of. A student might choose to show how being a competitive swimmer or a musician influences everything else in her life. Moving to a new place or having a particular relative or ancestor might impact a student's life significantly. The memoir definitely gives scope to this kind of single focus, while excluding other aspects of the writer's life.

Focused Instruction

Farha Shariff, a colleague of mine from the University of Alberta, leads students in a powerful prewriting activity for the memoir assignment. The activity also works for the students writing an autobiographical essay, and in fact, it is not necessary for students to have chosen a format yet.

Farha models a graph for students, showing them how the graph's vertical axis extends above and below zero, with gradations from 1 to 10 above and below zero. On its horizontal axis the graph shows dates from the year the student was born to the present. She shows students how to place events on the graph using words and/or symbols and pictographs that represent the best and worst things that have happened to them. Students are given a number of events (e.g., the eight worst and the twelve best) to plot.

10—the best   -10—the worst

Year	Above line events	Below line events

(Timeline graph, Form 22)

Scale above line (1 to 10), "10—the best":

- 10: I was born — We got 2 horses — I went to Germany
- 9:
- 8: We moved to the acreage
- 7: We got a dog — I got honors
- 7: My sister was born
- 6: We went to Disneyland — I went to a rock concert
- 5:
- 4: We moved to Stony Plain
- 3: I joined 4H
- 2:
- 1:

YEAR   1995 1996 1997 1998 1999 2000 2001 2002 2003 2004 2005 2006 2007 2008 2009 2010

Scale below line (-1 to -10), "-10—the worst":

- -1:
- -2:
- -3: I broke my arm — I started piano lessons — I had to take French
- -4: Mom started a job
- -5:
- -6: I failed my driver's test
- -7: I went to daycare after school
- -8: I got braces
- -9: Our colt died
- -10:

Independent Work

After students have seen the graphing process modeled, they create their own graphs in preparation for a sharing session with partners or small groups.

The graphs students create represent a wide range of artistry and reflection. Some students use only words, others only symbols, and many use some combination of the two. Some are carefully drawn and colored, some are inked neatly in black above the line and red beneath, and some are slapped down in pencil.

TECH TIP

Students can use Notebook to create these graphs for printing or presentation on a SMART Board. It is easy to select a graph format from the Gallery and then just type in the event. Symbols and graphics can be inserted with another click. An advantage of this format is the flexibility in rearranging the text and symbols on the page.

Similar graphs can be created using a graphic organizer. Once the basic graph is complete, it is possible to add levels to each box. For example, if "Trip to Disneyland" is listed, then clicking on the corner of the symbol opens up a new level in which the student can list some of the events and people connected with that trip. When complete, the entire document with all the information could be printed as a graphic, as an outline, or both.

Feedback

Students discuss their graphs in small groups or with partners. This is an important part of the prewriting process, where verbal processors gain better access to their ideas and where all students are encouraged by the interest of peers. Here, as students recall the events or the stories they have been told by their families, they get in touch with memories and expand their thinking about the events they have identified. As they hear from peers, some students are reminded of other events they can include or additional details that are important or interesting. Students typically increase their repertoire of ideas as well as their commitment to the writing as a result of this informal sharing.

Collaborate with students to create the evaluation rubric if this assignment is to be graded.

Creating a Rubric: Possible Elements for Memoir/Autobiography

- The title is interesting/fitting.

- An adequate amount of information is provided.

- The content is relevant (on-topic).

- The content is interestingly presented (specific detail).

- The vocabulary is precise, description vivid.

- The structure is sensibly ordered and sequenced.

- Sentence structure is varied and interesting.

- The composition is error-free.

- The composition is original.

- The presentation is clean/attractive.

You may wish to grade the graph separately from the written essay to recognize artistic students for their talent. If so, work with students to create a rubric for the graph.

> **TECH TIP**
>
> My students find using their mind maps an effective form for oral presentations. Because only the essential ideas are noted, students use their own memories to flesh them out as they present. The audience appreciates not having the autobiography/memoir being read to them.

Focused Instruction

Students who opt to write the memoir might benefit, depending on grade level and sophistication, from being walked through the frames for writing as they consider how to chunk and organize the events and details from their graph into paragraphs for the essay. (For more in-depth instruction on creating the body of the essay, see lessons on the literary essay on pages 72–80 and/or the persuasive essay, pages 80–88.)

Feedback

You may also wish to give feedback on a first draft to indicate whether writers have used a suitable organizational framework or if another one might work better. For struggling writers, the chronological structure of autobiography seems to work best.

If students are going to publish their essays in a collection or display them in any form, they will need an opportunity to have their work edited so they can make a finished copy based on those corrections. If students are delivering their material in an oral presentation, there is no need for this final, error-free draft.

Literary Essays

Middle schoolers are often asked to write essays that analyze or respond to pieces of literature. The practice of writing letters and personal essays strengthens my students' skills and boosts their confidence, and with that experience under their belts, they are willing to attempt more formal essays.

As always, samples of well-written compositions greatly help students to see what they are aiming for as they work on literary essays. The best models are past students' work, because the fact that their peers accomplished the task makes it seem more possible that they can as well. I save copies of every sort of composition for this purpose, but when I was just starting out I either had to find appropriate published materials or create a full or partial sample of an assignment myself to share with students.

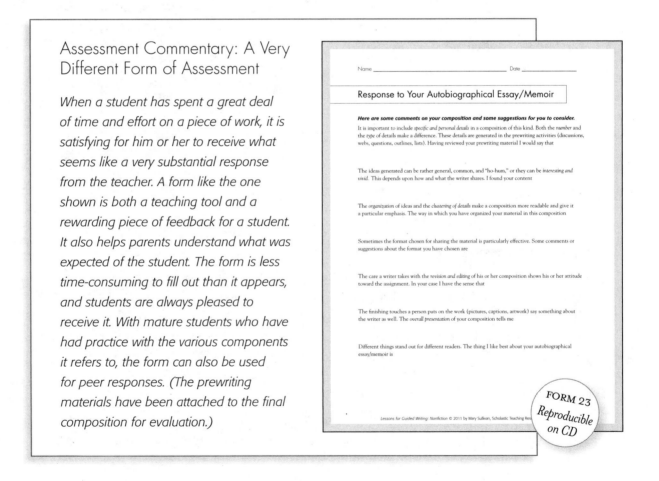

Assessment Commentary: A Very Different Form of Assessment

When a student has spent a great deal of time and effort on a piece of work, it is satisfying for him or her to receive what seems like a very substantial response from the teacher. A form like the one shown is both a teaching tool and a rewarding piece of feedback for a student. It also helps parents understand what was expected of the student. The form is less time-consuming to fill out than it appears, and students are always pleased to receive it. With mature students who have had practice with the various components it refers to, the form can also be used for peer responses. (The prewriting materials have been attached to the final composition for evaluation.)

Name _____ Date _____

Response to Your Autobiographical Essay/Memoir

Here are some comments on your composition and some suggestions for you to consider.
It is important to include *specific and personal details* in a composition of this kind. Both the *number* and the *type* of details make a difference. These details are generated in the prewriting activities (discussions, webs, questions, outlines, lists). Having reviewed your prewriting material I would say that

The ideas generated can be rather general, common, and "ho-hum," or they can be *interesting and vivid*. This depends upon how and what the writer shares. I found your content

The *organization* of ideas and the *clustering of details* make a composition more readable and give it a particular emphasis. The way in which you have organized your material in this composition

Sometimes the format chosen for sharing the material is particularly effective. Some comments or suggestions about the format you have chosen are

The care a writer takes with the *revision and editing* of his or her composition shows his or her attitude toward the assignment. In your case I have the sense that

The finishing touches a person puts on the work (pictures, captions, artwork) say something about the writer as well. The *overall presentation* of your composition tells me

Different things stand out for different readers. The thing I like best about your autobiographical essay/memoir is

FORM 23
Reproducible on CD

Lessons for Guided Writing: Nonfiction © 2011 by Mary Sullivan, Scholastic Teaching Res...

Assignment: Character Profile

For a character profile, I ask students to write an essay that describes and analyzes a character from a short story we have studied. Students have choices about the character and the story.

Focused Instruction

I want to teach students (and remind those who already know) that we need to gather evidence from the text to back up our interpretations of the characters we are investigating.

I remind them of the ways in which character is revealed in a short story: information can be given explicitly by the writer; by the character's thoughts, words, or actions; by what others say about the character; and by the ways others interact with the character. On the overhead, I display the text of a short story the class is familiar with and think aloud about why I am noting a particular quotation, incident, and so on.

I might model how to use one of the essay frames to help me generate and locate information. For example, as I search the text to gather evidence about Clarissa's personality, I might ask, *How does this character change from the beginning of the story to the end?* (a chronological frame of reference). Or I might ask myself, *What are the positive and negative aspects of her character? Or, How is Clarissa's inner self different from her outer appearance and behavior?* (questions from the opposites frame). Using the concentric circles frame, I might consider what I can infer about Clarissa from the way she acts when she is alone, with her family, with her friends, and at school. In some cases, I might not use any particular frame at all but just work my way through the story, jotting down details that help me understand the character.

When I've finished modeling, I show students the form they will use to record their notes—see the sample at right. (You'll find a blank template on the CD.)

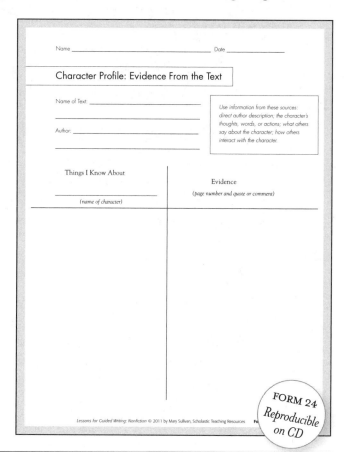

Designing Learning

It's important to keep in mind that some students will need an explanation about where we find evidence for the inferences and interpretations we make. In order to support many of the learners, I supply a note-taking sheet to remind them that they must first gather material before they begin to write.

For this activity, I like to use the "capture" feature of Notebook software on a SMART Board. The sample text can be captured and then projected on the SMART Board for the class to observe. It's a good idea to size the text to fit on the screen, but leave sufficient room around it for making notes. Once this object is locked on the screen, it is simple to write on it. While moving through the text with the class, make use of different pens (highlighters, creative, and so on) to note quotations and incidents. To further clarify the distinctions between each type of information, I might use the yellow highlighter to identify information given by the writer, green for information revealed by the character, and blue for information given by characters' interactions.

Scaffolding: Collaborative Practice

If you feel students need to practice with a partner (or that some students *wish* to), provide a short excerpt from a story and ask partners to work through the process of extracting information about the character and making inferences. When partners share their findings, students will be affirmed—or led—in the right direction before setting out to do this part of the assignment independently.

Practice

I invite students to choose a short story they've read and select a character to focus on. On the Character Profile form, students note the character traits and provide supporting evidence from the text, following the procedure you've modeled. If students will be using frames to guide their thinking, you may want to have copies available for reference. At this point, students fill out the Character Profile form as best they can. Collect these and select some examples to help you demonstrate the next step. Students are usually very willing

Since the frameworks are models I use frequently, I store blank templates in my Notebook gallery for use on the SMART Board. In this activity, I would have my text on the first page, then pull in a framework on the following pages. I can use the Dual Display and Pin Page features to display both the initial page with the text and the necessary framework page alongside it. Using the pens, I can jot notes on the appropriate page as we work through the piece. These visual representations make the process obvious to my students.

to allow me to use their work because they then have an advantage in the next stage. I use strong examples as well as examples that need some intervention/revision. I invent samples of what *not* to do when I think that will help.

Focused Instruction

Seeing how others have completed the Character Profile helps to reassure kids and broadens their own repertoire. I might choose the work of a student who has used one of the frames for writing or whose material lends itself to being framed according to one of the models we have learned. One student's work shows many opposites: Stella's inner person is shy, according to the evidence of her thoughts, but the student finds instances in which Stella acts boldly. The student says Stella is caring, and gives evidence of her private acts of kindness but says Stella behaves outwardly in a cold and hostile manner. We know from her thoughts that Stella wants to learn and be competent, but among her peers she pretends not to care. I might use this piece to show that the writer could decide to use the opposites framework to organize her essay.

Another student might give several examples of a character being very courageous. There may be enough material here for the student to organize an essay chronologically around various incidents from the story that show the character behaving courageously.

A third student may simply list several different characteristics with evidence, and I might ask students to suggest characteristics that "go together" so that I can recommend that the student use the categories frame.

Feedback

After this modeling, students can work in pairs or groups to help one another determine a workable organizational frame from their Character Profile form.

Focused Instruction: Introductions and Conclusions

Depending on the grade level and the level of sophistication of the terminology students are

TECH TIP

It is a simple matter to take the Character Profile form (available on the accompanying CD) and add it to My Content in the Notebook gallery for use on the SMART Board. Then it is always available when needed! If I've used the form to work through as a group activity, I can print the completed page to give to students who need the extra support of having that visual reminder right at their desks.

The research on learning styles shows that while some of us tend to see the "big picture"—trends and patterns—others are disposed to see the parts and the details. To write well we need both. Having students collaborate (when the purpose of collaboration is clear) can be very helpful. Peers should offer trends, categories, or frames they see emerge from the details, or conversely, encourage the writer to supply more accurate detail as evidence to support the judgments made about the character. Both sides of the Character Profile must be complete for students to move into the writing of the essay.

expected to use, you may want to review character types—dynamic, rounded, flat, and stereotypical—before beginning work on essay introductions. Make sure students understand that introductions act as signposts signaling to the reader what will follow. Because of this, a writer must know where he or she is going with a topic in order to write an introduction. In the literary essay, the writer has to have decided upon an interpretation of the character or the events that will be presented. To prepare for this, we have done the work of looking for evidence, trends, and patterns that arise from the notes we have taken from the story.

Students should work from their Character Profile forms (page 73) and their organization frame (if they've used one) to summarize their interpretation of the character and tell the reader what will follow in detail—e.g., *The text evidence I have found indicates that Isabel is a complex and interesting character who displays* . . . Some samples follow (pages 106–108) that illustrate exactly how these introductions look and function.

We also need to encourage students to think about *why* a writer portrayed a character in a particular way. How does it relate to the theme or message of the text? Thinking this way will help students formulate the main point they will convey in the composition, and may suggest ways to introduce the essay and wrap it up. Leading students in this type of reflection strengthens their critical thinking as they attempt to answer the *why* and *how* questions about the choices the writer made. This analysis also teaches them something about the craft of writing. Many students need to hear this "thinking out loud" to understand how readers make inferences and form judgments.

Here are some examples:

- The writer made me identify with Grace because he makes her believable and I feel for her in the situation. The characteristics he gave her made me like her and care about what happened in the story.

- The writer paints a very dark picture of Mr. Havers. The way he describes and portrays the character sets the reader up for thinking Mr. Havers is the thief.

- The writer shows us an angry teenager and we know even before it happens that Blaine will do something violent.

- The author presents a character who is kind of uninteresting at first. She shows the reader how weak and mixed-up Cynthia is at the beginning. That makes the story so good when we see how she changes after the vandalism at the party.

Scaffolding

Students often benefit from a chance to articulate what they think about their character in a global sense before they write their introduction. I might ask students to take their Character Profile forms to a group or partner discussion where they will each formulate a statement that sums up what they think of the character and why the portrayal "works" in the story. Students write better introductions and conclusions with this supported reflection.

- I think that Cole is portrayed as . . .
- This has the effect on the reader (or on the story) of . . .

Focused Instruction

Now I show students samples of introductions and provide suggestions about conclusions based on our general outline of the essay. I tell the students that naming the story and the author are always essential elements in a literary essay, and that the character name should also appear in the first couple of sentences. We will discuss together the degree to which the writers have pointed the way to what will follow in the body of their essays.

Introduction to the Literary Essay

SAMPLE 1

> Leiningen, the Brazilian plantation owner in Carl Stephenson's story *Leiningen Versus the Ants*, has a lifelong motto: *the human brain needs only to become fully aware of its powers to conquer even the elements.* Leiningen is a very arrogant man. There are many examples of his arrogance throughout the story as Leiningen brushes off warnings, and makes little of the knowledge and experience of the people who try to help him.

Looking at the sample together on the overhead/SMART Board, we discuss where we think this is heading. *What kinds of details*, I ask the students, *do we expect the writer of this essay to reveal as the essay unfolds?* Now I help them to articulate the order we predict the essay to follow. This introduction leads the reader into the evidence from the story that will demonstrate Leiningen's arrogance.

SAMPLE 2

> In Morley Callaghan's story *All the Years of her Life,* the author shows a teenage boy, Alfred, who shoplifts. Alfred finally realizes who his mother is and what she has been through. The evidence that follows here from the story will show that by seeing her, Alfred sees himself for the selfish and shabby person he is.

This introduction leads the reader into the examples of Alfred's selfishness and poor character as the essay writer details them.

After doing this activity a few times with students, I give them passages and ask them in pairs or groups to predict what the body of the essay will contain, based on the introductions. This practice activity does so much to prepare them for writing well. Without my having to mark anything, students receive practice and feedback from peers and from me. Breaking these complicated tasks into components and looking at them in isolated stages is both effective and wonderfully efficient.

SAMPLE 3

Sometimes an introduction that's *not* successful is instructive for students. Here is a nonexample.

> Filly for Sale *by Jan Graham tells about a girl who loves her horse. Carly has a horse of her own for the first time and she wants to train her as a jumper. Carly loves horses and is anxious to start training her horse as soon as she can. The problem is that she has to keep the horse at the neighbor's until the work on the corral is finished.*

Students clearly see the difference and can usually articulate why this is more of a story summary than an introduction to a character analysis.

Practice

Students work independently to create an introduction that shows the reader where they are headed with the essay. I give students an opportunity to meet with peers once they have actually written an introductory paragraph. Students often find that once they have established their direction, they need to revisit the story to beef up the evidence and examples to support the statements they're making about the character. (This is the recursive nature of writing in a nutshell, and when students recognize it, they have made an important discovery!) These samples are on Form 25 on the CD.

Feedback

I like students to hand in their introduction (with the Character Profile form attached) *before* they write the whole essay. If the introduction doesn't show any clear direction, I can conference with the student about the main message before he or she goes any further.

Focused Instruction: Transitions

One of my students called this organizational tool "transmission," and that is perhaps an illuminating misnomer because a transition really has to do with "changing gears" in writing. I tell students that transitional words and phrases connect pieces of text by leading us into a new idea, step, or paragraph. They signal a shift in the prose. In a composition with excellent transitions, the reader doesn't even notice the writer's skill because the text moves along so smoothly, like a car with an automatic transmission. If, on the other hand, transitional devices are absent or clumsy, the piece will lurch and hiccup like a car with a standard transmission that's being driven by a learner!

The transitional words and phrases refer back to an earlier point, stage, or step and connect what *came before* with what is *coming next*. You may want to give students a list of transitions like the one below. Additions can be added as you and students come across them.

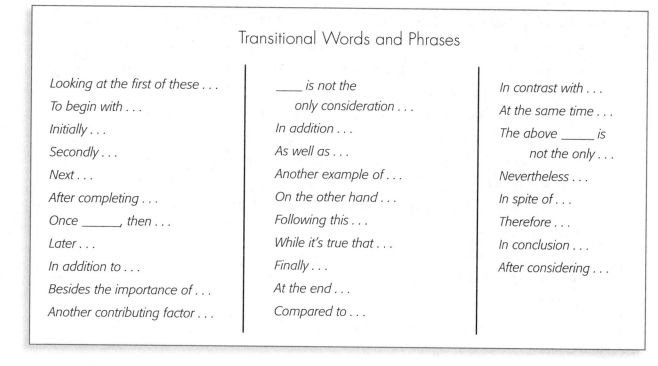

Transitional Words and Phrases

Looking at the first of these . . .
To begin with . . .
Initially . . .
Secondly . . .
Next . . .
After completing . . .
Once _____, then . . .
Later . . .
In addition to . . .
Besides the importance of . . .
Another contributing factor . . .

_____ is not the
    only consideration . . .
In addition . . .
As well as . . .
Another example of . . .
On the other hand . . .
Following this . . .
While it's true that . . .
Finally . . .
At the end . . .
Compared to . . .

In contrast with . . .
At the same time . . .
The above _____ is
    not the only . . .
Nevertheless . . .
In spite of . . .
Therefore . . .
In conclusion . . .
After considering . . .

Practice

If using transitions is new to most of your students, you may want to have them practice using them after you have first modeled the task for the class. Copy short essays (past student work is best if you have it) with the transition sentences deleted and have students in pairs or groups of three create transitional phrases or sentences that will connect the paragraphs smoothly. Share the results as a class, discussing why some choices work better than others. This kind of practice allows students to focus on a single element of the writing craft without having to deal with all the other challenges at the same time.

Note: Titles are discussed in the section on persuasive essays (page 80).

Independent Work

Once I'm sure students have a clear focus for their essay, they get to work on writing a first draft. This whole process is a much more hands-on approach than many students experience in classrooms where assignments are given and papers are graded. It is slower and more labor-intensive, to be sure, but students learn about writing because it isn't a one-shot event. Writers are exposed to (and part of) the hidden thinking, reading, and writing that go on behind the scenes in the heads of mature writers. As teachers guide students through the process year after year with this supportive approach, students become more willing and more able writers.

This might be a good place to work with students to create a rubric for the literary essay.

TECH TIP

To further develop transitioning skills, display student samples using the visual presenter. Then ask students to come to the board and use the highlighters and creative pens to highlight the transitional words and phrases.

Creating a Rubric: Possible Elements for Literacy Essays

- The title is interesting/suitable/relevant.
- The introduction clearly articulates the main thrust/theme/interpretation presented in the essay.
- The text references support the interpretation/viewpoint contained in the essay.
- The details are relevant and collected in coherent paragraphs.
- The details support/flesh out the interpretive statement/perspective stated in the introduction.
- The details and the paragraphs follow in a sensible order.
- Transitions smoothly connect the details and the paragraphs.
- Sentence structure is varied and interesting.
- Vocabulary is precise and descriptive.
- Conventions are correct.
- The conclusion sums up the points made.

Persuasive Essays

Students often have to write persuasive essays in content areas of social studies and science, as well as on standardized writing exams. To avoid the problem of plagiarism, I have students practice the persuasive essay based on topics they have firsthand knowledge of or topics about which they can gather information through informal interviews or surveys. Once students have learned to write the persuasive essay from scratch, as it were, they will have more competence with the format wherever they meet it.

Focused Instruction

Before we look at a particular assignment, I want to familiarize students with the format of the persuasive essay. We proceed much as we did with the literary essay. Students are given copies of a persuasive essay appropriate for their grade. (These essays are easy to find in most grade-level anthologies. Past students'

Name _____ Date _____

Analysis of the Persuasive Essay

Directions: Answer the following questions to analyze the characteristics of a persuasive essay.

1. What can you predict about the essay from its title?

2. What do you know about the perspective the writer has on this topic from the introduction?

3. From the introduction only, what do you know about the kinds of evidence the writer will present to support his or her perspective?

4. Read the first line of each paragraph after the introduction. What examples or details is the writer providing to support his or her argument? List one for each paragraph.

5. Read the conclusion and decide whether the writer sums up his or her argument effectively. In other words, is he or she convincing?

6. Do the facts and details presented support the opening perspective? Is the information accurate? Are sources cited? If so, are they reliable? Does the information refute the opposite viewpoint? How could you check this out?

7. Does the writer take into account the consequences of his or her viewpoint to members of other groups?

FORM 26
Reproducible on CD

Lessons for Guided Writing: Nonfiction © 2011 by Mary Sullivan, Scholastic Teaching Resources

Once students have completed the questions, they'll need to share their opinions. While discussing the responses as a group, an effective tool for engaging students in the discussion is using back-channel sites like TodaysMeet [http://www.todaysmeet.com]. While the conversation is taking place in the classroom, students can log on to a forum created by the teacher. When they have a reaction to a comment, they can type their response into the forum and have it displayed on the screen or interactive whiteboard. Students engage on different levels as suits their needs, while presenters have the opportunity to tailor their comments based on the feedback. At the end of the discussion, printing the transcript provides a record of comments. Prior to initiating a "back-chat," I want to make sure that students recognize what constitutes an appropriate comment for posting. We run through a trial session and clearly identify appropriate postings.

essays are ideal once you begin to collect them, and youth magazines or textbooks also contain such compositions.) In this lesson I have students do the analysis. As they read and discuss the essays (in pairs or small groups), they use the Analysis of the Persuasive Essay form to guide their thinking. I never have my kids attempt this alone because that isolates each student within the circle of his or her limited understanding and knowledge. In guided reading and writing, we keep trying to enlarge that circle by sharing the resources of the group and exposing students to the thinking of their peers.

I give students the following set of questions (included on the CD as a reproducible) to guide their analysis of the essay. Depending on the essays you use, you may want to modify these questions to make them more specific.

Feedback

Sharing students' analysis allows us to see how the writer first introduces his or her perspective and then "stacks up the evidence" in favor of his or her point of view, laying evidence out in the body of the essay and summing up arguments in the conclusion.

Assignment: From the Soapbox

Have students brainstorm topics of interest to them. Perhaps there are issues related to the kinds of food sold in the school cafeteria or vending machines, rules at home to do with chores or babysitting, regulations around sports teams, homework, or using skateboards at school. Whatever it is, students should pick something they feel strongly about, since their motivation will be stronger and their composition more convincing than if they really don't care much about the issue. (I find that this sharing of ideas opens up the possibilities for all kids. In the end, each student will be writing his or her own composition, so it matters little that students may write on the same topic.)

Focused Instruction

Most students will already have an opinion on the topic they choose. However, make sure to emphasize to students that when they thoroughly investigate an issue, they may discover information that causes them to change their minds. Remind students to be open to that possibility. If they change their thinking on the topic, their argument may end up being even more persuasive because of that!

The "research" students undertake as they gather facts about their topics will differ greatly, and that is as it should be, given the diverse levels of ability in the typical class. For some students, it will be as simple as asking for information and opinions from peers, parents, and teachers, while others may contact clubs or organizations and even look for material on the Internet. (Remind students who do Internet research that they must bring a copy of the information they accessed. This greatly discourages copying from the source texts.)

Scaffolding

I want to spare my students the agony of confronting a blank page when they approach a composition, and for that reason I always provide some form or device for generating and gathering material. I use the form below for gathering information for this essay (a reproducible version is found on the CD). Some students use the graphic organizers to help them get started, and I spend a few minutes demonstrating how those might be useful.

I pick a hypothetical essay topic: my opposition to the rule that in order to play sports at our school, students have to have good grades. Then I go through the form with students, discussing each question and filling it out with them as we go. I want to affirm the value of experiential knowledge and demonstrate that such knowledge has a legitimate place in their writing. I also want them to search out the facts and opinions of others and to weigh information and perceptions from these sources as they make up their minds and structure their argument.

I demonstrate how the frames of writing (see pages 62–65) might help a writer come up with material for writing. I might think aloud as follows:

Chronology: "Here we're reflecting on the element of time . . . birth to death, morning to night, beginning of the school year to the end. Does any of that suggest material for the essay about school sports?" Students might point out that in September the school has only last year's grades to consider and that doesn't give students a fresh start but rather punishes them and makes them miss the first sports of the year while they are trying to prove themselves.

Opposites: "I might think about having teachers make the decision about sports eligibility *before*, instead of *after*, the grades come in, and how using the sports as an incentive rather than a reward might encourage some kids to start doing their homework and studying so they can stay on the team."

Spokes on the Wheel: "I might think of the issue from the perspective of several different people. What would the parents say in favor of allowing all kids to try out for sports? What would the coaches have to say? Why might school principals be in favor of having even the poorest academic students play sports? What would psychologists and counselors think?"

Concentric Circles: "For this structure, I would consider how what's good for me as a student wanting to play sports might end up being good for my family, for the school, and/or for the neighborhood."

Categories: "Here I might list the three most important and compelling reasons every child should be allowed to play sports regardless of their grades in school."

Research-Based Persuasive Essays

For generalist teachers and subject specialists who want students to write persuasive essays based on research, the process is exactly the same as described above. Once students have found the appropriate information and made notes from their sources, the stages of development are the same. As a subject teacher, if I chose this format rather than debates, charts, or other graphic organizers for sharing the exploration of perspectives, I would use a curriculum-based topic and walk students through the process as the lesson above suggests.

This is a great time to make use of student response systems, also called "clickers." Many student response systems are on the market, including Promethean, Quizdom, and SMART Response. Basically, a student response system is a little device that lets students input answers to questions posed by a teacher on an interactive whiteboard or projection screen. The questions can be in multiple formats—True/False, Yes/No, Multiple Choice, Multiple Answer, or numeric. (Think of watching the studio audience vote for their favorite clip on *America's Funniest Home Videos*.) Using these technology tools is powerful because they immediately tabulate student answers, so I can display a graph or chart (my choice) illustrating the range of responses. Once a topic is chosen—such as Mary's essay topic of *students need good grades to play sports at school*—pose a question, such as *True or false—students should have good grades in order to play school sports* to the class, and ask students to identify which side they support. Once students have had the opportunity to research the issue, write, and share their essays, present the same question again. The students can't wait to see the graph and results—and what better way to demonstrate the power of the written word!

The schools in our city were asked to provide suggestions to a task force on the environment. Our class wrote about the benefits of riding bikes to school and ways the city could make this easier. Our submissions were chosen for presentation to the city council, and in recognition we were given a prize of a class pizza party or a $200 donation to an environmental charity of our choice. Immediately upon being given the news, we used our clickers to vote on our choices, and the pizza party was the majority's favorite. Students then wrote persuasive essays about their choice and presented them to the class. Once everyone had the opportunity to listen to the various reasons, the clickers came out again. The power of their words was evident in the change in the graph, as the majority now chose to support the environmental charity.

Should 45 pick the pizza party?

Yes

No

No (38%)

Yes (61%)

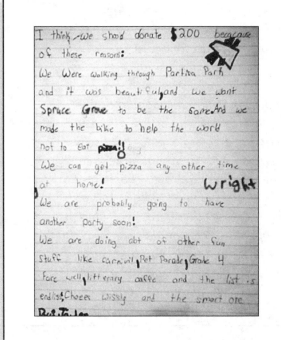

I think we should donate $200 because of these reasons:

1. We were walking through the Participark and it was beautiful, and we want Spruce Grove to be the same. We made the bike to help the world NOT to eat pizza!

2. We can get pizza any other time at home!

3. We are probably going to have another party soon!

4. We are doing lots of other fun stuff like carnival, Pet Parade, Farewell, Literary Café and the list is endless.

5. Choose wisely and the smart choice.

—By Jayden

I think the charity is the right decision to do because:

1. We want Spruce Grove to stay green.

2. We can get pizza at home!

3. The Mayor doesn't want us to help the environment by eating all the pizza we can. He wants us to raise MONEY for the environment. That was the whole idea of the activity!

4. Pizza is a silly thing to spend $200 on.

5. Pizza is useless.

6. Spruce Grove is our home. That's something to spend $200 on.

7. It can help change the fact that there is too much garbage.

8. Spruce Grove is much more important than pizza.

Come on, 4S! Charity needs it!—By Chantal

I put a lot of thinking into others' decisions but I changed my mind after hearing Kane's story. I said "Wow! He's right!" Our green areas are disappearing and we can put a stop to that ourselves. Simple but it doesn't seem to be that simple. Besides our earth is dying and becoming a giant hazard. That's why I say we need to try to put more green areas into Spruce Grove. There are lots already, but we need more because sooner or later those areas will start disappearing. We should take the $200 for charity and try to end that cause. Don't make a scene—be green.

—By Callum

Now that you have listened to what your peers have to say, think carefully and make your choice.

Should 4S pick the pizza party?

Yes

No

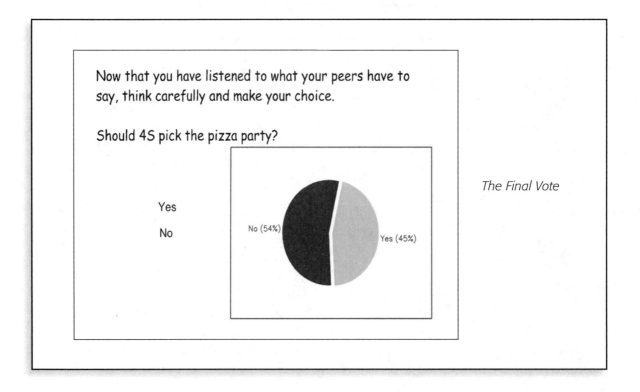

No (54%)   Yes (45%)

The Final Vote

Lessons for Guided Writing: Nonfiction © 2011 by Mary Sullivan, Scholastic Teaching Resources

A Word About Titles

A mini-lesson on creating titles will help students think of interesting and effective titles for their compositions. Brainstorming terminology relevant to the topic, thinking of related sayings, and considering the essay's main message will all help to generate ideas. Students should help one another with suggestions. For the school sports topic discussed in this lesson, some examples might be the following: Schools Need to Play Fair, Give Every Kid a Shot, When "A" is for Athletics, Sports for Sport's Sake, Academic Politics and School Sports, Failing to Make the Team. *Reports, unlike essays, tend to have titles that* label *the contents directly the way headlines do:* The Decline of the Red-Tailed Hawk in Montana *and* How to Keep Your Dog Healthy. *The difference between the two types of titles is analogous to the difference between* Green Bar Soap *and* Irish Spring.

The more we use these frames, the more students use them as techniques for generating ideas for writing and as organizing frames for compositions.

Practice

As students begin to fill in their forms, an opportunity arises to share their beginning efforts. Doing so encourages progress and helps those who need to "see it" in order to do it, which is why I sometimes share student work that I see is going in the right direction. Students can also work in groups of three to assist one another until at least some of the parts of every student's form are filled in. Sometimes, having simply *begun* means they've overcome the biggest hurdle.

The rest of the process of working on these essays is the same as the work on the literary essays (see pages 72–80). Both require an introduction and a conclusion that students formulate in a similar process.

Assessment

Sometime after the students have gathered information but before they begin to work on a first draft, a rubric should be created that clearly shows students what an excellent persuasive essay will look like.

> **TECH TIP**
>
> By this time, my students are familiar and comfortable working with graphic organizers. They will naturally turn to the software to assist them with their research. Mary mentions the obstacle of the blank page—it always amazes me how the students who are frozen by that page are able to generate ideas when building an electronic mind map.

Creating a Rubric: Possible Elements for a Persuasive Essay

- Amount of information
- Quality/accuracy of information
- Persuasiveness of the argument
- Variety of sources
- Effectiveness of the title
- Strength of introduction and conclusion
- Sensibly ordered supportive detail/evidence
- Precise vocabulary
- Control of conventions
- Neatness of presentation

The Essay on Standardized Exams

In many states and provinces, students are required to write standardized exams that include writing fiction and nonfiction compositions in various formats. In Canada, students are often required to write a personal or persuasive essay. Prompts vary, and in some cases no prompt is supplied.

When I know students will simply be given an essay topic without prompts, I prepare them by encouraging them to use the frames for writing to help them to generate material for the composition. I suggest that they use personal experience and anecdotal evidence wherever that is appropriate because it gives them material with which they are familiar and about which they are knowledgeable.

If students are required to write about leadership, for example, they might draw on their experience on a sports team. If the topic is peer pressure, students can share their personal experiences. It's more important for students to practice the *approach* to the essay and the ways to connect the topic to personal experience than it is to practice writing whole essays.

I can only give meaningful feedback to a limited number of essays, so students would not improve substantially even if that was all I did. But if I use our time to show them how to confront exam topics, over and over—to think about the relevance the topic has to something in their lives—and if I show them how to plan ways to structure such an essay, it *will* make a difference to the level of skill and confidence they bring to the task.

Students who have been walked through the process with in-class essays will be able to move out from those supported experiences into the new territory of the exam essay. It's important to use the kind of question that students will encounter and to show them how they can connect their experience to the topic in a relevant way. Once students have generated material, they will be wise to structure it using one of the frames with which they have had practice, since strong, cohesive organization really separates the successful essays from the rest.

The Picture Prompt

In some cases, students are required to write an essay from a picture prompt. I try to prepare them in three ways. First they need to systematically examine the picture(s) from top to bottom and from left to right, quickly jotting down everything they see and any response they have to it. Many students, in their nervousness, miss important aspects or details of the picture prompt, and while there is no one right answer with a written response, it certainly helps for a student's response to relate directly to the picture. This activity of covering paper with words also gives students a sense that they are beginning to address the task. It overcomes the blank page and helps ward off exam jitters that leave a student feeling he or she "can't think of anything."

Secondly, I teach students to refer to a handful of concepts or themes we have discussed and memorized. (These will depend on their grade level.) For middle school students, I work with concepts like *change, conflict, isolation, contrast,* and *celebration.* I have the students view the prompt picture and refer to their jotted notes to see if any of these suggest a theme to write about. One exam picture showed part of the city of Berlin with a family's walled garden in the foreground and huge cranes all over the city behind it. Another showed a group of Hawaiian girls and one white girl dancing in a circle holding hands. Students begin with the picture and move to a theme they can connect with it.

Finally, I remind students of the frames for writing and suggest, when possible, they structure their ideas using one of these frames to give it organization and coherence. The practice students have had working through the components of the literary essay and the persuasive essay help them immeasurably in dealing with these kinds of exam tasks.

TECH TIP

When working with picture prompts, my classes love to use the Storybird Web site. Users can choose a topic, and view pictures and art related to that subject, or alternatively browse through a wide array of art for inspiration. The art is superb and truly has something for everyone. Once students select the artwork, it is simple to add text and create a storybook with professional results. When published, the project can be viewed by anyone with an Internet connection, which allows family and friends to view and comment on the work.

Evaluating Exam Practice Essays

If your students write standardized essay exams, introduce them to the scoring rubric that the exam assessors use. Go through it with them, showing them what each category includes and discussing what excellence in that category would look like. These scoring rubrics are usually available to teachers. If the rubrics are not available, you might use the rubric the class has created for the persuasive essay. In any case, these will be very similar to the criteria you have been using with students throughout the year.

Conclusion

The essays in this chapter require little research except for the literary essay, which requires students to review a piece of literature for evidence. This chapter has a twofold message for teachers:

1. Design prompts and discussion that will generate rich material for writing

2. Teach and demonstrate the use of frames for thinking and writing

The next chapter looks at the kinds of nonfiction writing that will support students as they undertake research. For students, mastering these functional forms of both reading *and* writing is essential to their success as researchers. Locating, gathering, and recording information with efficiency and accuracy precede any and every formal writing task based on research.

CHAPTER 5

Conducting Research: Functional Nonfiction Writing

In keeping with the guided writing approach of my teaching, I have separated the conducting of research itself from writing a research report for three fundamental reasons:

1. I want to focus on the nonfiction writing skills students need to locate, generate, and record information that they will require in academic and personal situations.

2. I want students to enjoy the excitement and challenge of gathering information (of learning), free from the anxiety and reluctance that many students feel about writing a report or an essay.

3. I want to teach writing and research skills without having to contend with plagiarism issues.

Gathering information is itself an arduous task when it is done with thoroughness and care. Students will find rolling up their sleeves and hunting for information easier when they undertake it as a group, and if they aren't dreading what they have to do with the information when they find it! In fact, the same body of information we amassed together on a given topic can be incorporated later with any or all of the genres we intend to teach. If, for instance, we decide as a class to find out everything we can about the great northern dog-sled contest the Yukon Quest, students have an opportunity to practice the research skills of searching, reading, and recording. In subsequent lessons on sharing information, we can use that common body of knowledge to create alphabet books, letters, news articles, posters, oral presentations, and, *yes*, even essays and reports!

Kinds of Research

Our pedagogical objectives for having kids engage in research determine how we conduct our lessons. When I want students to do subject-based research when we're working on biographies, I will ask the school librarian to bring in a block of biographies that cover a range of subjects and reading levels. I'll check out the local library for a list of titles. For younger students, Kelli recommends generating a list of appropriate Internet sites searched out in advance. I will show and tell students how I made these arrangements. This may include a session demonstrating the use of the library computer's database. It may involve showing them how I entered certain prompts on Google to find sites pertaining to famous individuals and to biography as a general subject. Although this part is in effect *my* research, it shows students my process for investigating a topic. I want students to broaden their notion of resources and see that people are also sources of information—parents, teachers, members of clubs and societies, and staff at colleges, museums, planetariums, and science centers.

If, on the other hand, I want to show students the broad range of materials available on a very specific subject, I might choose a topic such as the mountain grizzly bear and bring in a variety of sources of information, including several reference books, photography books, wildlife reports, hunting magazines, and copies of *National Geographic*, as well as a list of related Internet sites.

It's important to show students that the *purpose* of doing research often determines the scope of the search or dictates the kind of resource you need. Some research we do is purely exploratory: *I'm interested in the trap-door spider because we talked about it in science class. I want to know more about it*. At other times, the purpose of our research is to locate the answer to one or more specific questions we have. The purpose of research ought to, at times, expand or limit the search we undertake.

> **TECH TIP**
>
> Using electronic formats makes the sharing of research easy. It's possible to use formats that allow all students to contribute their work and save it for later use. The format can be as simple as a shared Word document or an online forum such as PrimaryPad.

> **TECH TIP**
>
> A simple way to access people sources is through e-mail. Sending an e-mail request to a contact person at an institution usually yields a wealth of information, or at the very least, a suggestion for another contact. I encourage students to use several sources and send multiple e-mails to maximize the chance of a positive response.

Before students begin to investigate any topic for any purpose, it is important that they know what it is they seek to answer, discover, understand, or document, and for what purpose. Even when we are gathering information to serve as a collective pool for later compositions, we can identify types of specialized detail and an inclusive scope of information that will provide us with what we might need for our subsequent compositions. Teaching students about determining the purpose for research is also one of the first steps in freeing them from the grip of the source text; there's no point in copying whole sentences and paragraphs that do not answer the focus questions we have established to guide our research.

Accommodating Differences

Students have different learning styles, and these come into play when students do research. Certain individuals have a preference for opening things up. They like to explore and ask questions. Others have a predilection for nailing things down, for finding answers. There tend to be fewer of the former types than the latter, but both preferences are valuable. Explorers like Christopher Columbus are examples of the former type. I had Ryan, his modern counterpart, in my fourth-grade class.

Given the assignment of researching and writing about an animal that interests him, Ryan read his way through a dozen books on spiders, alligators, Siberian tigers, and Komodo dragons. He had made some notes on most of these animals and had thought about four different ways of framing his report, which was due the next day.

Thomas Edison wanted to make electric lights, and he stubbornly labored, testing several hundred substances in his search to find the one that would work to create light in a bulb. Suzy is a young version of such a destination-oriented doer. She knows from day one that she will write a report that explains why bunnies' eyes are pink. She has done the title page, made the notes, and returned the book to the library.

Kids who are very destination-oriented need to be pushed to explore a little so they won't simply latch onto the first topic they think of, and kids who are very exploration-oriented need to be forced to narrow things down to a specific focus. Both activities are important parts of research—the opening up to many possibilities, and the closing down to move to completion.

Suzy needs to be encouraged to open up the possibilities for investigation and the final product. Ryan needs a deadline for his exploration, at which point he needs to narrow things down and zero in on one aspect to create an eventual finished product. As educators, we need to see both preferences as strengths, and we need to help each student gain the attitudes and strategies to make the most of his or her particular preferences.

I like integrating the use of graphic organizers into research topics because the program can accommodate both the destination-oriented and exploration-oriented children. Once students have generated their notes as a mind map, I usually have students color-code their topics (a very easy task). The mind maps show by color whether the student has generated many topics and no detail or a single topic with many details. As I walk around, without even reading the words, I can tell by the colors whether they have narrowed the topic down or not. I also know what kind of intervention is needed. Suzy has narrowed the topic too quickly and Ryan has not even chosen a topic to pursue. As a class, we can produce examples of both types of organizers and decide how many topics are enough and how many details are sufficient (generally a range for both) as part of our criteria.

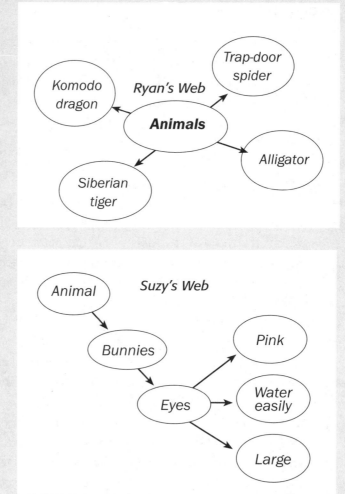

Focused Instruction: Purpose Statements

This first step for students—determining and stating the purpose—is critical in shaping their efforts toward a successful conclusion. Without this narrow focus, readers can find themselves browsing through materials that, although interesting, are not pertinent to the research. Students can waste a great deal of time looking at resources without really knowing what it is they want. Practicing ways of defining a purpose before the actual search and before the creation of any product is valuable. I show my students the following purpose statements and walk them through the formula below; each statement should include the purpose, the format of the product, and the intended audience.

- I am doing this research to find out about the labors of Hercules for sharing through an alphabet book.

- I am doing this research to prepare for an alphabet book on monsters of Greek mythology.

- I am doing this research to learn about the Golden Fleece and share the story through an alphabet book.

Students create a purpose statement by asking themselves *why* they're going to do research: Why am I doing this research? (The answer should have a **verb** near the beginning.)

- I am doing this to *learn* . . .
- I am doing this to *explore* . . .
- I am doing this to *find out* . . .
- I am doing this to *prove that* . . .
- I am doing this to *compare* . . .
- I am doing this to *contribute to* . . .
- I am doing this to *prepare for* . . .

The rest of the answer should specify a form and an audience, as well as the specific topic or question.

- . . . to learn about the life of the Micmac so I can defend their interests in the debate.

- . . . to explore the possibilities of different outcomes to the French-English conflict for our class discussion.

- . . . to prepare for writing a letter from the point of view of a king's daughter.

- . . . to find out the recycling depots in the community for a brochure I'm creating for residents.

- . . . to show that the gas plant near the school produces potentially dangerous emissions.

A Note About Purpose Statements

When your students are working to create any kind of research-based written product, they must structure their purpose statements as focus questions. The focus questions reflect the criteria for the content of the composition and describe the content part of the rubric. They help you clearly define what you want from your students and how you will measure their success.

Depending upon your students' grade level and time restraints, you may provide these questions for students or create them together as a class. If you wish to include certain non-negotiable elements of the assignment, this is a place to spell them out. Focus questions for a study of an explorer might include the following: When did the explorer embark on this journey? What prompted him to explore new lands? Where did his travels take him? What hardships did he encounter? What new information did his travels bring to light? What does history credit him with? What were some of the outcomes and implications of his discoveries?

Practice

I present my students with a list of subjects and ask them in pairs or small groups to generate research purpose statements. This activity helps many students finally understand what it means to limit the topic, where, in the past, they were satisfied to say, "I'm doing the rattlesnake."

Feedback to the whole group is easy to provide by sharing their statements on the overhead.

Reading Skills for Research

Students often need some perspective on the ways in which reading for information differs from reading for pleasure. I engage in some discussion with students about how we suspend disbelief in order to enter the world of a fictional character when we read a novel, but activate our critical faculties when we read for information. The whole discussion around fact and opinion has never been more important than in this information age. In the arena of technology, Kelli has some important tips for us as we teach kids to consume information with intelligence and caution. Besides being able to identify indicators of legitimate sites, students need to be aware of indicators within language itself that help us separate fact from opinion.

Students also need to be taught about close reading and rereading, as opposed to skimming and scanning. We often take for granted that students know how and when to read in different ways, but many students, even at the high school level, do not fully recognize the different types of reading we do for different purposes. Some students, particularly struggling readers, remember being told to read every word and not to skip over any when they are reading, but rather to sound them out. These students need our encouragement—even permission—to read in a different way. I've found that having trouble reading is one reason for the struggle and reluctance some students have when it comes to research. They are overwhelmed by the task of plowing through large amounts of print. For these students, seeking out particular information from a body of text can feel like searching for a needle in a haystack.

This is why practicing certain skills as a single focus *before* taking on the comprehensive projects that require them is so crucial. I work with students to help them see the need for reading critically and employing diverse reading skills *before* they need them for actual assignments.

Focused Instruction: Critical Literacy

In this activity, I guide students in checking the reliability of sources and the validity of information.

PREPARATION

Gather (or create) short texts and label them with source data, including the date, the name of the writer (or label "anonymous"), the institution or company, and where the text appeared (the ad section of a newspaper, on a billboard, in a pamphlet, etc.). The texts need to be at an appropriate grade level, but this can be done successfully with students from grades 5 and up. You might include excerpts from a letter to the editor, a newspaper

---

TECH TIP

Students must be taught to consider the source of information when looking at Web sites. Checking the suffix on the URL address can be a first step when distinguishing between fact and opinion. A ".com" ending means that the Web site is used for a commercial purpose, which may influence the content. Organizations are represented by ".org," and information on the site may be biased by the group's point of view. Universities use ".edu" and are likely to be current and supported with additional references. A good source for additional information on domains and country codes is 2Learn.ca's Top Level Domains and Country Codes (http://www.netknowhow.ca/nkhSRcc.html).

A useful exercise is to model evaluating a Web site. Try using the worksheets provided by 2Learn.ca at http://www.netknowhow.ca/nkhSREvaluate.html available for use online or in printable format.

---

column or editorial, a science encyclopedia entry, a news article, an outdated text with stale information, a current government report, an anonymous piece, and an advertisement. If you are creating these samples, especially for younger students, there need only be excerpts of two or three sentences, since it is largely the source information that will give them clues to evaluate the reliability of information.

The first time I had students participate in the following learning activity, I had to do some additional work, but once I had the material in place, it continued to be an effective tool. For one such lesson, I gave my ninth-grade students the assignment of locating samples of various kinds of texts on a given topic, labeling the sources, and commenting on their value and reliability. I later used these texts (in whole or part) to set up the following activity for seventh graders.

Scaffolding

How are we to know that information is reliable? I ask students. I distribute the same numbered pieces to all groups/partners with instructions to read the pieces and rate them from most to least reliable. It's wonderful to witness the rich discussion that happens among students as they point out characteristics of the various texts and make suggestions as to why one text might be more reliable than another.

Once student groups have ordered the pieces from most reliable to least, they post their lists on the wall or the board. Then a speaker from each group defends and explains the group's ratings. This activity greatly raises students' interest in the criteria we use to judge the reliability of information because they now have a vested interest in defending their group's assessment.

Focused Instruction

After such an activity, students express more interest in my going through their pieces with them and discussing aspects of reading critically. We discuss the possible purposes of the various writers. I point out that writers' perspectives are shaped by their motives. Information found in a travel brochure, for example, is less likely to be purely factual than an article in a reference book, since the travel brochure has a purpose to entice people to visit, whereas a reference book is more likely to present the straight facts and leave conclusions up to the reader. If an article is in the news section of the paper, it is unlikely to present an opinion (except in a quote identified as such), whereas a piece on the paper's editorial page will undoubtedly express opinion. If the source of the article is not named, we have good reason to question the information itself. If a doctor is quoted in an advertisement, she has less credibility on the topic than if she is quoted in a medical research journal. In most cases, the more recent scientific and statistical information is, the more accurate and trustworthy it is.

Another aspect of critical reading is to pay attention to what is omitted from the information presented, or what is marginalized by placement on the page, font size, and other such factors. A newspaper with a political bias can underreport positive aspects of one political party's activities and give plenty of press to events involving the party they favor.

Editorial decisions about the amount of coverage topics receive and about the placement

Lessons for Guided Writing: Nonfiction © 2011 by Mary Sullivan, Scholastic Teaching Resources

of the articles in the paper are examples of this kind of influence. Whether an article appears on the front page or is buried in a back section affects the exposure the information receives and also makes a statement about the importance of the information. In a third world country's report about new schooling regulations, the fact that the article mentions only the advantages for boys gives the message that the education of girls is not important.

Language often gives us strong indications about whether a text is based on fact or opinion. I provide students with the following information as a handout or on a chart in the classroom (see the CD for a reproducible version). In itself, this form is not a task but a handy guide that might be used to analyze a text to discern whether it is fact or opinion. A practice test of statements could be created where students first have the handout available as they decide whether a statement is fact or opinion. A subsequent independent test without the guide could measure students' grasp of the concepts.

Guide to the Language of Fact and Opinion

- Point of view and wording are clues to whether a fact or opinion is being expressed. Opinions may begin with a direct admission of what they are: *In my opinion . . . I feel . . . I think . . . It seems to me . . .*

- Imprecise language is a clue that the material may not be factual: *Many people say . . . Some people conclude that . . . It is considered to be . . .*

- Fact, on the other hand, is almost always supported by a reference. *In the work done by . . . The Meteorological Bureau of London reports that . . . Local census figures show . . .*

- Sometimes opinion is passed off as fact in persuasive writing. Statements are made that sound like facts but sources are not identified. *A reliable source reports that . . . It is well-known that . . . Our sources show . . . Research tells us that . . .*

Name _____ Date _____

Guide to the Language of Fact and Opinion

Point of view and wording *can be clues to whether a fact or opinion is being expressed. Opinions may begin with a direct admission that they are indeed opinions.*

- In my opinion . . .
- I feel . . .
- I think . . .
- It seems to me . . .

Imprecise language *is a clue that the material may not be factual.*

- Many people say . . .
- Some people conclude that . . .
- It is considered to be . . .

Fact, *on the other hand, is almost always supported by its* **reference.**

- In the work done by . . .
- The Meteorological Bureau of London reports that . . .
- Local census figures show . . .

Sometimes opinion is passed off as fact in persuasive writing. Statements are made that sound like facts but sources are not identified.

- A reliable source reports that . . .
- It is well-known that . . .
- Our sources show . . .
- Research tells us that . . .

Lessons for Guided Writing: Nonfiction © 2011 by Mary Sullivan, Scholastic Teaching Resources

FORM 28
Reproducible on CD

Focused Instruction: Skimming and Scanning

I want students to understand that close reading and rereading are ways that we clarify material and extract precise detail from text passages. *Skimming* and *scanning*, on the other hand, are ways of surveying a large amount of text very quickly for certain purposes. Using examples on the overhead, I show students these different reading techniques.

I explain that when I am looking to answer a particular question, I scan a text, visualizing

TECH TIP

Several years ago, I answered a knock on my classroom door to find several visibly upset students, petition in hand. They had been alerted to a Web site that promoted the creation of "Bonsai Kittens" by imprisoning kittens in glass jars at a young age, complete with instructions. Angered by the descriptions and pictures of mistreatment of animals, they decided to begin a petition campaign to force the site off the Internet and were going throughout the school collecting signatures.

While wanting to encourage the girls' willingness to take action, I told them I needed more information before signing their petition. After just two minutes on the Web site, it was obvious that the creator had his tongue firmly planted in his cheek. He had managed to take photos of his kittens crawling into some glass jars and used his writing skills to create a believable scenario for "preserving the long lost art of body modification in housepets."

This was a wonderful opportunity to show my students how to recognize that not all the information found on the Internet is believable. We examined the site and discussed the characteristics that demonstrated its legitimacy, as well as the tip-offs to its insincerity. I also introduced the class to the Snopes Web site (http://www.snopes.com), a reliable Internet source for checking the authenticity of Web sites, e-mails, urban legends, and more.

Students need to recognize that posting information on the Internet is incredibly easy, and more than ever they need to carefully consider the source of the information. Using examples of Web sites like Bonsai Kittens (http://www.ding.net/bonsaikitten) or the failure of the California Velcro crop (http://qualityshows.wordpress.com/2010/04/16/from-the-archives-failure-of-velcro-crop-threatens-hungarian-economy/) gives them the opportunity to practice essential skills for verifying information.

the shape and size of the target word. My eyes sweep the page, moving left and right. If we want to know who won the dogsled race in 2004, we might first scan for the date, because numbers stand out in the text. In a table of contents, we are searching for key words. In an index, we are scanning to the letter range in the alphabet first and then to the term we are seeking.

Skimming, another quick, survey kind of reading, involves paying attention to titles, headings, and introductory and concluding sentences. Skimming a text gives me the general drift of the information. I might skim through an article to see if it makes reference to the aspect of a topic I am interested in—Is there anything in this piece about how they train dogs for the race? Or I might skim an article to summarize the point of view—Is the writer in favor of raising the minimum age for driver's licenses or not? Skimming helps us decide if a particular text is helpful and warrants closer reading, or if it can be cast aside.

Practice: Skimming and Scanning

I have students practice skimming and scanning through timed search activities administered by a partner. Over time, if you make tasks of varying lengths and levels of difficulty, students can challenge themselves by advancing to the more difficult search tasks as they get better at skimming and scanning. (I create the exercises using whatever class sets of books are available, literature or otherwise, to cut down on photocopying. Again, older students or strong students can also create their own such activities for use with the class.) The *scanning* questions simply ask students to find a certain word, number, or answer to a question. The skimming questions ask them to answer global types of questions about the excerpt. The excerpt used can be an index, table of contents, or page of text with graphic information as well as print.

For some struggling readers these lessons are a revelation! *No one ever told them they didn't have to read it all.* The skills they acquire make their subsequent confrontations with text less intimidating; somehow it feels like less is asked of them than when they are assigned to read an article, for example.

> **TECH TIP**
>
> Using an interactive whiteboard assists with skimming and scanning practice. Find a suitable Web site with appropriate information for the topic. When practicing scanning, have students identify the key words by highlighting them or using the floating tools. A magnifying tool enlarges the selected words, and a spotlight tool focuses on the key word while still allowing the rest of the page to be seen.

Practice: Locating Information

Now I want students to put together the skills and knowledge they've gained about locating information from texts (including electronic texts). I don't want to grade and respond to essays when I am teaching students to access information, so I assign a set of research challenges that they work on in pairs. The questions can be open-ended (finding what they judge to be reliable sources) or require specific right answers, such as the focus questions they will encounter in subject-specific research. Recording precise information regarding sources should also be part of the task. Providing students with a format for their response always lends practical support. Research done without plagiarism issues! The essay writing happens at another juncture.

Writing Skills for Research

Just as there are reading skills that students need when they do research, there are also a number of functional writing skills that students use to record and manipulate the information they glean from research. It may be that we write notes from texts we encounter. We summarize material for different purposes. Taking notes, summarizing, making charts, and creating graphic organizers are all useful ways to record information for study purposes or to use in later formal writing. Although they are never seen by another reader, these skills can be extremely important components of the writer's success in other communication tasks. To help students master them, we need to provide instruction, scaffolding, practice, and feedback.

It is generally helpful to create a list of suitable Internet resources before introducing them in class. It is a worthwhile investment of my time to spend an hour finding useful Web sites, as opposed to having students spend two classes searching and not finding anything concrete. Once I have a list of sites, I might list them in a Word document and save it in a shared folder for students to access. Alternatively I may decide to have students retrieve the list from an Internet page (especially useful if I want them to continue working from home or after class time). There are many Web sites that allow you to create a quick and easy page. Filamentality (http://www.kn.pacbell.com/wired/fil/) is a tool that lets me select from several different formats to build a page. The step-by-step, easy-to-follow instructions provide me with a successful resource page for students to use. One drawback can be a long URL for students to have to type. Using the TinyURL Web site lets me customize the Web address to a shortened form. Another useful site is the My Desktop@2Learn.Ca tool, which lets me quickly create lists of sites, as well as activity pages using my designated sites (http://www.2learn.ca/mydesktop/howtos/wismydesktop.html).

This class search for information is an excellent opportunity to teach Internet searching skills. Before beginning I want to prepare students for the unexpected. They must know what to do if they end up on an inappropriate Web page. I want them to 1) close the page and 2) come tell me. There is always a chance that an innocent search can yield an inappropriate page, and I want the students to have practiced the steps to minimize consequences.

We start with some basic skills, and discuss the importance of using a reliable search engine such as Google. I demonstrate how using quotation marks limits the results to pages that contain just that phrase. For example, *chocolate cake* yields results for *chocolate* and for *cake*. Using quotation marks around the phrase narrows the results to just my favorite dessert. I also demonstrate how using a "+" sign or a "–" sign attached to a word ensures that the word is in the results, or removes that word from the pages. (If I want fudge icing, I could use *+fudge*. If I don't want walnuts, I could include *–walnuts*.) I remind students to choose their search terms carefully, and we practice developing specific terms. Generally, using more words yields better results. We discover that looking at the results can give us new ideas for rephrasing the search. I show students how to evaluate the choices (using some of the previous tips for evaluating Web sites, such as URL endings). Once students gain these skills, they are less likely to spend hours searching with little to show for their efforts.

Note-Taking

Showing students how to make notes and "fact cards" from text sources that they locate in their research is a skill that precedes the sharing of information in any format. I have students do this apart from the actual assignments of research and composition. It's the skill that connects the two. A textbook from science or social studies is great to use for practice because all students have one.

Focused Instruction: Making Fact Cards

I talk out loud as I make fact cards from the text, projected by an overhead. These cards contain key words—nouns, verbs, numbers—rather than complete sentences. Let's say I'm gathering information about Peter the Great from an article that I won't have access to later. I tell students that I want to jot things down as if someone else will have to make sense of the notes. I do this because, in fact, once I no longer have the original text in front of me, I can't be sure I will know what I meant and the notes will be of no use to me unless they are clear.

First I write "Peter the Great," then "notes from." Here I will name the text (or site) along with the publisher, year of publication, and the page number. One of the problems with notes, I point out, is that sometimes they are written without clear headings, which makes them hard to identify after a lot of notes have been taken on different aspects of the topic, or from different sources.

I continue to think aloud. *"The key facts here are the date 1703, when Peter the Great started building the city of St. Petersburg, the location, and the fact that the people suffered great hardship to build it."* I write "St. Petersburg: [I double-check that I have spelled it correctly] *started 1703 / Mouth of Neva River / swamps and forests."*

I read from the article, "Serfs, including women and children, were conscripted into labor battalions to build the city." I pause and think aloud. *"What does* conscripted *mean? It seems like they were forced. I should put that in so I'll remember the term in case I have to know it."* I write *"People and kids forced (conscripted) to build city."*

Progressing this way, I model creating notes based on the paragraph in the text. We discuss the benefits of doing this:

- I know what the notes refer to and where they are from.

- I have the key facts.

- I have clarified meaning while I have the *context* of an unfamiliar word.

- I have double-checked numbers and spelling so I won't have to look them up again later.

- I have enough of the information to still be able to make sense of it later.

Practice

In small groups or with a partner, students read an assigned paragraph or section of the text and come up with the important information by creating fact cards for that portion of the text. When this task is complete, I have students write a paragraph based on another group's fact cards (I do *not* tell them about this portion of the assignment when they're taking the notes). Students often have difficulty working from another's notes because the writing on the fact cards is hard to read, the notes are vague, details are separated from the context, or language is used that is not understood. These problems are exactly the difficulties we run into with our own research notes if any time has passed and we're separated from the original text.

TECH TIP

Using a visual presenter and/or interactive whiteboard gives every student a front-row seat to the action. You can capture a piece of text to work with, then reframe it and jot notes on it.

Using a graphic organizer at the beginning of the note-taking process readies the information for later use. The format of the symbols (circles, ovals, and so on) makes it difficult to fit in large chunks of text. This limitation forces students to focus on the essential facts and information.

Feedback

The task provides instant feedback about what works well and what creates problems with note-taking. Students might rate on a scale of 1 to 5 the effectiveness of the notes they worked from. They can use the five benefits of good note-taking listed on page 103. Groups can talk about what, in particular, created difficulties for them as they wrote their paragraph.

Independent Work

If you plan to use some researched material to create other nonfiction pieces at a later date, this would be a good time for students to create notes from sites or text materials you have selected. Have students create fact cards for a broad topic such as Greek mythology, or some curriculum-based topic in another subject area. Later you can use the material as content to try some of the genres that appear elsewhere in the text. This way students practice researching and note-taking and at the same time they create a resource that you can use in the future. All this happens without your having to grade essays and without students having to resist copying the found text! Remind students of the importance of double-checking numbers, facts, and spelling for accuracy. Insist that students be careful in recording the exact source of information—including publisher and year of publication for books, and for journal or magazine articles, volume, issue numbers, and dates.

Note-Taking From Non-Text Sources

Sometimes student research involves listening to live or videotaped oral presentations. The ability to listen critically and take notes from an oral presentation is an important skill in many academic and work contexts. The note-taking form on the next page can be modified for use with a documentary or a television program that provides in-depth coverage of an issue. The purpose of this activity is to demonstrate to students the benefit of thinking about a topic before listening to a presentation.

Focused Instruction

Before watching a video or a presentation, I go through this form with students and show them that mental preparation for note-taking is like the predicting and questioning we do when we read with attention. As the presentation is under way, we can listen for answers to these questions.

Note-Taking from a Video or Presentation

Read and think about these questions before you view the presentation so that you know what you are looking for.

1. What seems to be the purpose of this presentation (to inform, raise awareness, persuade, entertain, thank, introduce, and so on)? Is there any other agenda? How do you know that?

2. What main points are raised in the presentation?

3. What details, evidence, or examples does the speaker use to illustrate these points?

4. What conclusion, solution, dilemma, or impression does the speaker end with?

5. What information is expressed through the nonverbal aspects of the presentation?

Name _____ Date _____

Note-Taking From a Video or Presentation

Directions: Read and think about these questions *before* you view the presentation. Read the questions again immediately *after* the presentation and fill in as much as you possibly can under each section. These notes can be brief—key words and phrases—as long as you can understand what you wrote.

1. What seems to be the purpose of this presentation (to inform, raise awareness, persuade, entertain, thank, introduce, and so on)? Is there any other agenda? How do you know?

2. What main points are raised in the presentation?

3. What details, evidence, or examples does the speaker use to illustrate these points?

4. What conclusion, solution, dilemma, or impression does the speaker end with?

5. What information is expressed through the nonverbal aspects of the presentation?

Lessons for Guided Writing: Nonfiction © 2011 by Mary Sullivan, Scholastic Teaching Resources

FORM 29
Reproducible on CD

Practice

Ask students to take notes from a video or presentation. Have partners compare and expand their notes and then meet in groups of four and finally in groups of eight to discuss their notes and their differing responses to the presentation.

Further Relevance of Note-Taking Skills

These functional writing skills help students in their ability to closely read texts in content areas of social studies and science. They enable teachers to divide up the work of reading whole sections of material, and to have students make study notes. Once students have learned summarizing, they can use it the same way to divide up certain texts and to condense information for study purposes.

Teachers often assume that students possess these types of nonfiction writing skills. When I worked at the high school level, I was dismayed to see how many students lack these fundamental functional writing skills. Yet I find that once students see their peers' strategies and share in a successful collaborative activity, they can soon manage the same task independently.

Writing Summaries

As with other mental processes, the business of summarizing is not something crystal clear to all students. Some wonder where a summary comes from, how a writer decides what goes into one. If we want students to be able to write summaries for a variety of purposes, we need to teach and let them practice the skill. This lesson may seem too juvenile for middle school students, but summarizing a paragraph is often more difficult than summarizing an article, where an introductory paragraph and introductory sentences make the job easier. I like to explain the concept of summarization with a very short composition, which is easier for students to follow in shared reading than a lengthy article. This is simply a demo, I tell the kids, but the approach is the same even with an article or a book. This little walk-through takes the mystery out of summarizing for kids who just don't get it.

Focused Instruction

I select a text that is below grade level so that students can focus on the process and the concept without any trouble understanding the gist of the paragraph. The following script gives a general idea of how I proceed.

"Beginning to make a summary is like looking into a bag of text and asking some questions about the contents.

"What's in here? Be quick now. I'm only going to give you a peek." I place a text about cats on the overhead for only a few seconds. I don't want anyone to be able to read the whole paragraph.

"So, what's it about?" The students say "cats." We start by naming the subject of the text. This lets almost everyone in and encourages participation because it seems obvious and easy. I then place three or four other paragraphs of more sophisticated text on the overhead very briefly, asking the same question. What's in this bag of text?

It's about Russia. It's about elections. It's about plants. It's about earthquakes. I purposely make it very informal at first. Even struggling students' reactions indicate that this may be doable. That was easy. You didn't have to use any fancy vocabulary. You didn't even have to read it all!

Now I replace the original paragraph about cats on the overhead and ask students to read the text carefully and decide how to answer the next question: "What kinds of things does the text tell us about cats?" We progress to considering what the details have in common. It's important to say *kinds* because I don't want them to list all the details. That's what kids who can't summarize do. I want them to figure out what the details have in common; I want them to describe the category that all the details belong to. This is a critical component of summary.

If students answer with a specific detail, I tell them I want to know what it is that every detail is referring to. What can you say about all the details? What *kind* of information do they tell us?

"They tell you how to look after a cat," the students say.

"And what is it that the text says is important about all those things?" We finish by making a statement that sums up what the text says about that whole accumulation of related details.

"It says that if you have a cat, you should look after it properly."

We are almost there. Now we go back to the important *ways* to look after a cat properly.

"They should keep it clean and healthy and make its life happy," someone else offers.

"Great! Now that you have shown me what is in this bag of text, we need to make a clear and complete statement of those contents."

And this is what we come up with: *This paragraph describes how cat owners have a responsibility to look after their cats by keeping them healthy and happy.*

OR

This paragraph tells the reader that people who have cats should keep them clean, well-fed, and healthy. They shouldn't have a cat if they don't have the time and concern to treat it well.

Independent Work

FOR BEGINNING SUMMARIZERS

To summarize long sections of text, students should work in pairs or groups of three in their first efforts. One method of providing feedback and support is for students to start in pairs and then join another pair and finally make a group of eight. Each time the group expands, a reading of the summaries takes place and the new group rewrites the summary in a way that the participants agree improves the summary. The three or four large groups then share their final summary with the class. This activity allows the weaker students an opportunity to engage in the work supported by stronger peers. It also allows students to hear the metacognitive activity usually going on only inside the heads of capable students.

Students often need help categorizing the details in a paragraph. It is helpful to give common category labels, such as *characteristics, suggestions, descriptions, causes, tips, consequences, outcomes, results, reasons,* and *problems.* You may want to model categorizing details several times, pointing out that the introductory paragraph of the piece often contains category labels.

FOR OLDER STUDENTS

For older students, a good discussion and learning opportunity takes place when pairs or groups examine two summaries—a successful one and a poor one made from the same article.

(These summaries are quick to create and make an excellent teaching tool. The weak summary can proceed disjointedly, have factual errors, miss main points, include too much detail, fail to sum up the message of the article, and so on. Students often find it easier to identify what's wrong than to describe what works.)

After a close reading of the two summaries, the group should discuss the following factors: statement of the key message or thrust of the article, inclusion of the main points of the article, inclusion of details (relevant and irrelevant), the order of details in the summary, the treatment of conventions, and the overall appearance of the composition. The group should then create a rubric by articulating the characteristics of the excellent summary. Students could then use the resulting criteria as checklists for assessing their own summaries and/or those of peers.

Creating a Rubric: Possible Elements for Summaries

- Presents statement of the key message/thrust/main idea of the article briefly and concisely

- Presents the main points of the article accurately, briefly, and concisely

- Includes only important and highly relevant details

- Orders material sensibly to reflect the article's structure

- Is free of errors in conventions

- Is neat and clean

> **TECH TIP**
>
> Displaying the two summaries on an interactive whiteboard or with a visual presenter simplifies this process.

Conclusion

The reading and writing skills required to do research are often taken for granted at every grade level. When *are* they taught? If we assume that students possess these skills when in fact some do not, those students cannot enter the learning with dignity. These students sense that such skills have not been addressed because one is already supposed to know how to proceed, so they feel that they shouldn't ask or show their ignorance. This gives these students license to pull back and drop out of the activity, since they do not possess the entry-level skills. All students can use a quick refresher and can participate in collaborative activities that allow them to show leadership and give support to those in need of it. Real investigations also require students to make use of nonfiction writing skills. These will be practiced in the following chapter.

CHAPTER 6

Real Investigations and Nonfiction Writing

If we hope to create scholars of our students, we must replace our concern about covering the curriculum with a desire to show students how much there is still to be uncovered, recovered, and discovered. There are infinite questions to be asked, an unlimited number of investigations and explorations to be undertaken. It is through engaging in this type of research that students learn to be purposeful observers and to look at the world with genuine curiosity.

In order to do active research, students may need some further functional writing skills. They may need to make careful observations and describe things with precision. Their research may involve the posing of questions to gather certain baseline data and to conduct interviews or surveys. These are also skills that need to be learned and practiced.

Real investigations can be as simple as having students report on the care of a pet. Their research could involve having conversations with family members or other people who own pets. They might talk to a local pet-shop owner or veterinarian. Students might contact an animal shelter to gain information and perspectives. In this chapter we'll look at creating effective interview questions and useful surveys to generate and collect information for student essays.

A field trip can be a real investigation if students are charged with gathering certain kinds of information. A local custom or venue could be the subject of the investigation. Any building or cultural event in the neighborhood could serve as a topic for research.

Recording Observations

Many students' writing across the genres suffers from a combination of insufficient detail and the use of imprecise detail. Writers often describe things in the kind of general and

A field trip can occur without getting a single permission slip signed or riding on a yellow bus. Virtual field trips online are the next best thing to being there. To accompany a unit on Shakespeare and Elizabethan England, my class visited the fully reconstructed Globe Theatre in England. We stood on the stage and were able to look around 360 degrees to imagine the actors' points of view. Another class was able to step inside the Iroquoian long house of the Turtle Clan. As we moved through the building, students observed firsthand the sleeping arrangements, spiritual symbols, and food preparation and storage. Googling "virtual field trips" yields millions of hits. Many sites have organized lists of links to virtual field trips, such as the Utah Education Network site http://www.uen.org/tours/fieldtrips2.shtml.

Another electronic version of a field trip is a video conference. Video conferences link two distant sites together and allow real-time communication and interaction. Video conferencing equipment is widely available, but a video conference can occur simply by using Skype or Google Talk. Since many computers have built-in webcams, using Skype or Google Talk is as quick as registering and getting the free download.

Zoos, museums, businesses, and research and science centers all have developed programs for delivery via videoconference (called content providers). Imagine diving in the Great Barrier Reef and examining marine creatures, or being part of actual surgery in real time! As powerful as these paid programs are, I relish the opportunities provided by video conferencing to develop leaders among the students. As experts on the area in which we live, my students have presented information on our region to students throughout our province, as well as peers in California, Louisiana, Egypt, and other countries across the globe. We have learned about writing from author Marty Chan, creating Ukrainian Easter eggs from the third-grade class in a neighboring school, and building totem poles from a British Columbia artist. While studying the history of Alberta, we were told the stories and customs of First Nations people in our area from second-grade students in another school in our division. These experiences would simply not have been possible as regular field trips.

vague vocabulary that passes in informal conversation—*It was great. It was awesome. It was gross*—but that doesn't do the job in formal prose. Formal writing of every kind demands that writers render a fuller and sharper picture. Whether students are writing a lab report or a descriptive essay, they need to use all their words. As teachers, we tend to think that perhaps students do not have the vocabulary to do a better job, but that is almost never the case, except with second-language learners.

Focused Instruction: Attribute Listing

Years ago I stumbled on the concept of attribute listing, and I have used it ever since to show students how to access the very broad vocabulary they have to describe things.

I use concrete objects to start with—two drinking vessels: a baby bottle and a thermos, or two photographs of the sky: one dark and cloudy, one sunny and clear. I ask students to look at the two objects and tell me ways they differ. Students are not allowed to say, "One is made of plastic and the other is made of metal." They have to say, "They differ in the material they are made of." As students list attributes, I put them on the board, each as the head of a column. Students will say (sometimes with the help of questions and cues from me) *They differ in function, purpose, cost, size, color, shape.*

Once we have several attributes listed, I ask them for specific words under each column. *"What else can drinking vessels be made of? Think about ones used on picnics or at formal occasions. What about mugs, tea cups, paper cups, thermoses? What are they made of?"* Under the "material" column for drinking vessels, I write *glass, plastic, wood, paper, china,* and so on. These are the specific words that describe this particular attribute.

We do the same exercise with words for *sky. What are the attributes for "sky"?* Students with more or less prompting at different grade levels will come up with categories like *time of day, time of year, weather, color, size, place, mood, temperature* and *contents.* Under these headings (attributes) they generate words like *dawn, November, winter, rainy, gray, broad, Kansas, tranquil, angry, dismal, cold, searing, jet-streaked, bird-filled.* (Sometimes we start this as a class activity, and once they see how it works I give pairs or groups the columns of attributes, and we hold a contest to see who can come up with the most words in each category.)

When I have demonstrated to students that they own many, many precise words for describing things (and have not looked any of them up in a thesaurus), they seem genuinely surprised. Why do I never see them write *under a November sky* or *under a cold sky?* How about *an empty sky* or *a deep sky?* Kids know these words. They know them well and can use them appropriately. They need to be shown the repository of language they have and how to access this language when they write.

Attribute listing is useful for students in any writing activity, including planning research and seeing the scope of possibilities for generating or gathering information. *What are the attributes of birds and which of these are we interested in describing in our reports on birds of different kinds? What are the attributes of team sports and how can we use them to chart the differences between these two sports? What are the attributes of heroes that we can refer to here?*

Attribute listing is a technique that students can use in many instances. I can sometimes quickly help a student who is blocked by referring her to the technique once she has experience using it.

Note-Taking in the Field

If we plan to require students to write about a field trip experience or if students are gathering information and impressions for a writing project based on research at a local site, for example, we need to have them prepare to notice and record particulars. When we ask them to write about the experience after the fact, we lose the opportunity for some great description and original insights.

A local middle school used to hire me to go to camp with their students to do writing sessions with them. I would create a writer's notebook that asked them to engage in certain prescribed writing activities and make notes about a variety of things they would see and experience. When the students returned home from camp, I would go to the school to help them turn their journal notes and writing exercises into formal pieces of writing. These became poems, alphabet books, acrostics, news articles, and letters. Without the campers' notebooks, these pieces would have lacked much of the vividness and clarity they expressed.

Many, if not all, students will benefit from support in capturing information when they visit a site or witness an event. Students require a framework for catching information, and/or for reflecting at the end of the day (or at specific intervals) about the things they saw and experienced. Such guides greatly enhance students' access to the raw material that leads to richer compositions and fosters independence on subsequent projects.

Relevance: What We Know, What We Learn

Engaging students in a discussion before the field trip, finding out what they know and what they want to learn, is a way of heightening the relevance of the experience and of the subsequent learning.

Scaffolding

Prepared students can glean more from observations and field trips, so it makes sense to help them start thinking before they go. If students know quite a bit about what they will see and do on a field trip, they can utilize an open form with headings that match the schedule of the day. You might use a simple form like the one shown at right; you'll find a reproducible version on the CD. Have students read the questions ahead of the trip itself for the same kind of mental preparation discussed concerning the video presentation. With younger students, talk in advance of the trip about the *kinds of things* they might record.

Lessons for Guided Writing: Nonfiction © 2011 by Mary Sullivan, Scholastic Teaching Resources

Even if I haven't experienced a particular field trip before, I usually have a general idea of some things to expect. I've found that giving students questions before the trip and having them write their answers based on their current knowledge creates a strong focus for the actual event. I have the class redo the questions on the day following the field trip to give them an opportunity for reflection and time to show what they know.

This is a great time to make use of student response systems, or "clickers." I like to save the answers and graphs from the original question session to compare and contrast with the responses following the field trip. Although it is easy to create and ask factual questions ("Which of the following animals are found in the Boreal Forest?"), the most dramatic differences occur when I pose opinion questions ("Would you like to move with your family to the Boreal Forest? Explain your answer."). When there are noticeable differences in the before-and-after graphs, we have rewarding discussions analyzing the variations.

Student engagement always soars when we take out the clickers. Since students know we will be redoing the activity the following day, they are quick to note applicable information during the field trip. They are also likely to ask focused questions if answers haven't been supplied during the field trip activities.

Notes for a Field Trip

1. List several things particular to this site or event that you noticed.

2. What did you see that surprised you? Why?

3. What did you find particularly interesting or impressive? Why?

4. Did you learn about an interesting person? Describe him or her.

5. Was there a part that was sad or moving to you? Explain.

6. What do you know now that you didn't know before the trip?

7. What are you left wondering about?

8. What makes this an important place/event in our community?

Name _____ Date _____

Notes for a Field Trip

1. List several things particular to this site or event that you noticed.

2. What did you see that surprised you? Why?

3. What did you find particularly interesting or impressive? Why?

4. Did you learn about an interesting person? Describe him or her.

5. Was there a part that was sad or moving to you? Explain.

6. What do you know now that you didn't know before the trip?

7. What are you left wondering about?

8. What makes this an important place/event in our community?

9. If you could be (or could have been) involved in this place/event, what part would you like to play in the place or in its history?

10. What difference does this place/event make to life in your community?

Lessons for Guided Writing: Nonfiction © 2011 by Mary Sullivan, Scholastic Teaching Resources

FORM 30
Reproducible on CD

9. If you could be (or could have been) involved in this place/event, what part would you like to play in the place or in its history?

10. What difference does this place/event make to life in our community?

Interviews and Nonfiction Writing

Interviews are a great way for students to gather information for a variety of nonfiction writing projects. Students might interview the school principal to write a news article for the school paper. They might interview a new teacher in order to introduce him or her over the PA system. Students might interview a scholarship winner or an award-winning athlete to create a poster for the school pride board. They might interview senior citizens to write essays about what these people's lives were like in another era.

Focused Instruction: The Interview

Most students will have little experience with interviews except what they've seen on television sportscasts and talk shows. This is an excellent opportunity to demonstrate what an important role purpose and audience have in writing. An interview that is conducted

TECH TIP

Remember, there's more to technology than just computers! Telephones are a powerful technology tool. Many of the phone systems installed in schools allow for a call to be placed on a classroom intercom. If the intercom is not available, I use a phone with a conference call button. Before sending students to complete small-group or independent interviews, I usually have the class develop a list of questions for a particular individual. Depending on the class, I either select or ask for one or two volunteers to conduct the interview over the phone in the classroom setting. To ensure success, we have a class rehearsal and role-play the different parts and possible answers. Then we call the interviewee and get started. (I have previously spoken with the interviewee to arrange a suitable time, and tell him or her that the interview will be a broadcast event.) This experience is successful because it involves everyone in the interview, if only as an audience member. Having the class nearby provides support for the interviewer, and we can whisper encouragement or write hints on the whiteboard as the interview progresses. When the interview is over, we debrief and discuss what worked well. Now everyone has an idea of what to expect, and all are more likely to be successful in their independent interviews.

My junior high students interviewed their parents and grandparents when we wrote essays for the province's 75th anniversary. Writing these essays, students had to learn how to generate and gather information through interviewing. They had to explore ways to shape the information in sensible and effective ways. The students had their compositions published in a local paper, and they were paid for their writing!

to gain information about an event or a person for the purpose of creating a written text, whether of the interview itself or of the material collected from the interview, will be a very different encounter than the interviews students see on television.

When students prepare questions for an interview, they will need to create focus questions similar to those they create for other research. An important difference to stress is that with interviews, their questions will elicit new information so the questions themselves will determine the kind of information that will be generated.

Another difference is that the interviewee is in control of the information he or she will provide, and for that reason, the courtesy and demeanor of the interviewer affects the outcome as well. An individual being interviewed may open up more to a person who has clearly prepared for the interview, who listens and responds with genuine interest, and who is warm and courteous.

Tips for Creating Interview Questions

- Ask questions that will elicit the specific information you want to know.

- Prepare questions and comments that demonstrate you know something about the person or event.

- The best questions ask for information and interpretation or perspectives on key information.

- If you use questions that can be answered with yes or no, follow up with a request that the interviewee elaborate on the answer.

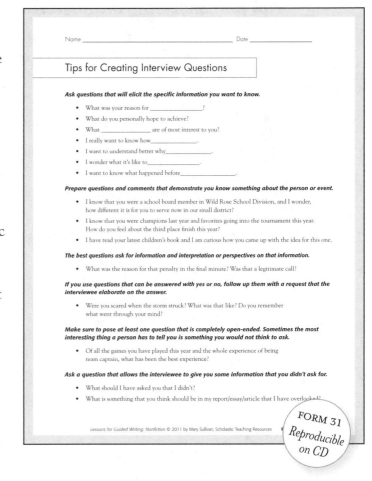

Name _____ Date _____

Tips for Creating Interview Questions

Ask questions that will elicit the specific information you want to know.

- What was your reason for _____?
- What do you personally hope to achieve?
- What _____ are of most interest to you?
- I really want to know how_____.
- I want to understand better why_____.
- I wonder what it's like to_____.
- I want to know what happened before_____.

Prepare questions and comments that demonstrate you know something about the person or event.

- I know that you were a school board member in Wild Rose School Division, and I wonder, how different it is for you to serve now in our small district?
- I know that you were champions last year and favorites going into the tournament this year. How do you feel about the third place finish this year?
- I have read your latest children's book and I am curious how you came up with the idea for this one.

The best questions ask for information and interpretation or perspectives on that information.

- What was the reason for that penalty in the final minute? Was that a legitimate call?

If you use questions that can be answered with yes or no, follow up them with a request that the interviewee elaborate on the answer.

- Were you scared when the storm struck? What was that like? Do you remember what went through your mind?

Make sure to pose at least one question that is completely open-ended. Sometimes the most interesting thing a person has to tell you is something you would not think to ask.

- Of all the games you have played this year and the whole experience of being team captain, what has been the best experience?

Ask a question that allows the interviewee to give you some information that you didn't ask for.

- What should I have asked you that I didn't?
- What is something that you think should be in my report/essay/article that I have overlooked?

Lessons for Guided Writing: Nonfiction © 2011 by Mary Sullivan, Scholastic Teaching Resources

FORM 31
Reproducible on CD

- Make sure to pose at least one question that is completely open-ended. Sometimes the most interesting thing a person has to tell you is something you would not think to ask.

- Ask a question that allows the interviewee to give you some information that you didn't ask for.

Feedback

Once students have created their questions, have them meet with peers and use a checklist or rubric (made with the question tip sheet in mind) to ensure that they have created appropriate questions for the interview.

Focused Instruction: Conducting the Interview

Discuss with students the aspects of the actual encounter that might be difficult. I go through the list below and hand it out to students. A reproducible version is found on the CD.

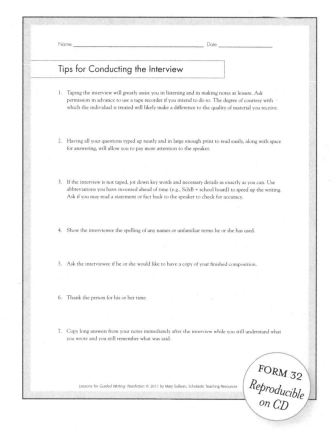

Tips for Conducting the Interview

- Taping the interview will greatly assist you in listening and in making notes at leisure. Ask permission in advance to use a tape recorder if you intend to do so. As mentioned before, the degree of courtesy shown by the interviewer will have a notable effect on the quality of material you receive.

- Have all your questions typed up neatly and in large enough print to read easily, along with space for answering, which will allow you to pay more attention to the speaker.

- If the interview is not taped, jot down key words and necessary details as exactly as you can. Use abbreviations you have invented ahead of time (e.g., SchB=school board) to speed up the writing. Ask if you may read a statement or fact back to the speaker to check for accuracy.

- Show the interviewee the spelling of any names or unfamiliar terms he or she has used.

- Ask the interviewee if he or she would like to have a copy of your finished composition.

- Thank the person for his or her time.

- Copy long answers from your notes immediately after the interview while you still understand what you wrote and you still remember what was said.

Practice

It helps students feel confident in the process if they can practice their questions with a partner. Partners should invent answers to the questions so the interviewer can practice note-taking, which is especially difficult for younger students.

Independent Work

One choice is for you to select from questions that your class has created for an interview that will take place in front of the students (with a staff member, coach, local politician, member of a club) and have a student conduct the interview. The interview is taped, and all students take notes to the best of their ability. After the interview, students work in pairs/groups or independently to construct a summary of the information discussed in the interview. Students then check their information against the taped interview to see if they missed any important information.

No matter how you have students use the information from interviews, students will benefit from the experience of creating questions and conducting the interviews. Students might not produce a formal written composition but simply use their notes to tell a partner what they learned from the individual they interviewed.

Students who use a tape recorder can transcribe the interview and present it with a partner, who reads the interviewee's part. If your teaching objective relates to the gathering of information and not to a formal written product, you could assess students by having them reenact the interview from the transcript, without grading the written part at all.

Depending on the genres your students learn this year, they might use the information from the interview to create a news article, summary, essay, or report. If students are writing essays from their notes, it might be useful for them to revisit the writing frames to see if these suggest an organization for the material. A rubric would then reflect the criteria for that particular genre, as well as the specific aspects of content required in the assignment. Students might simply meet in groups to relay the information they gleaned to peers. In an ensuing discussion, students could identify the aspects of their experience that were successful, enjoyable, problematic, or difficult.

Conclusion

The main learning in this chapter is about how to become more effective and efficient in capturing, collecting, and recording material from nontext sources. Whether students use the materials for subsequent discussion purposes or to form the content of a piece of written work, the important learning will be about how they can prepare themselves to carry out such observations and recordings more successfully. The practice of these tasks is more important than the resulting product or performance. For this reason, peer and class discussions about the experiences are an essential element. Writing from research, the topic of the next chapter, is in some ways easier—after all, it's all there in black and white—and in some ways more difficult, because, after all, it's all there in black and white!

CHAPTER 7

Writing From Research:

Using Research Material to Create Original Texts

When I want students to share information they have gained through text research, I have them do so using genres and formats very different from the source material. Using these legitimate and often overlooked types of nonfiction writing teaches students to manipulate information, and it allows them to gain familiarity with writing in a new format. In the beginning I did this to circumvent the "copying" issues discussed earlier, but as I continued to use these formats I recognized other benefits, not the least of which was opportunities for students to experience having their original work read and responded to by authentic audiences. (Material copied from other sources is seldom received with the same delight and appreciation that original texts elicit.)

We have already seen how letters and news articles can be used in imaginative ways, allowing students to convey what they've learned from social studies and science content. Among other formats I have used, the alphabet book is a favorite. Posters, strip stories, and oral presentations all allow students to think about information and reshape it in novel ways. The mental interaction with the material that such reshaping requires helps students learn the material more fully than sharing information in a format similar to the source text, which is almost akin to moving information from the source to their own paper without it passing through their minds at all!

Sharing Information Through Alphabet Books

The alphabet book is a challenging and interesting format to work with. Many published writers have used this format, and plenty of books are available to use as models at various grade levels. Bringing samples from literature to show students is helpful and motivating. Samples of previous *student* books, once I had collected some of these, are even more motivating for students because they see what it is possible for writers at their grade level. I have seen alphabet books based on particular animals, on communities studied, on early explorers, even on chemistry and math terminology, to mention just a few.

Individuals, small groups, and the entire class can create alphabet books. A colleague sent me an alphabet book (created as a whole-class project) called *Light and Shadow Alphabet* that was a fourth-grade science project. A shared book like this can be the practice project before small groups or individuals take it on. It meets the curriculum content objectives for science while serving as collaborative practice for the new genre.

Focused Instruction

As with the introduction of any new genre, the first part of my instruction is modeling, and I do this by sharing excellent finished pieces. When students see the possibilities for content in the text and graphics, they become enthusiastic about the project. A careful look at various alphabet books is a good starting place. If the project is meant to carry important subject content, then students should look at examples that contain factual information.

In groups or as a whole class, depending on the age and maturity of learners, analyze just how successful these books are at conveying facts and new information. If the proposed content is part of your required curriculum study, you would set criteria that outline the content that must be included in the finished products. You can also create these requirements together with students. If, for example, you are studying certain communities, you might specify that the book must contain information about the following areas: land features, industry, resources, occupations, activities, and weather. For animals, the directions might be something like this: the alphabet book must provide a physical description of the animal, information about the young, and a description of its diet, habitat, and enemies.

Even walking older students through the stages of gathering information for a book like the one they will create is helpful. In the example of the social studies project, I pick a community other than the ones the students will be choosing, and we work on it collectively.

Scaffolding: Modeling the Search for Information

For the social studies research on communities, I choose Iqaluit, capital of the newest Canadian territory, Nunavut. Every piece of writing begins with the writer stockpiling the

---

Requirements and Choices

At first, when I gave students a choice between writing a report and making an alphabet book, they invariably chose writing a report. I learned that a new genre has to be taught and practiced students will choose it. (It becomes a real choice only when students know how to do it.) I have had students from grades 2 to 12 create alphabet books. Once students are well versed in the characteristics of a new genre and have collaborated on creating such compositions, they find it challenging and interesting to experiment with it.

kind of material that Canadian writer W.O. Mitchell called "rough lumber." Students search for items under the various criteria. They look at textbooks, pictures, library books, atlases, and Internet sites for information about the geography, climate, and activities of life in Iqaluit. I post the alphabet on the board and/or place separate letters on chart paper around the classroom, along with alphabet sheets at students' desks. The richer this base collection of facts, the more interesting the resulting book will be.

I show them that when necessary they can use any part of speech, including prepositions, to begin their page. For the letter *I*, for example, a page might begin with:

- In winter . . .
- Isolated . . .
- Ice fishing . . .
- Inuit . . .
- Icy waters . . .
- Inhospitable climate . . .

Scaffolding Through Collaboration

Allowing students to work in a group to collect facts means that weaker readers can participate—they might find items in pictures and scan for words beginning with a particular letter. In this gathering phase, we might use a graphic organizer like the one below to ensure that students gather information about all the required topics. For the communities project, we start with finding terms for geography, climate, and activities of life by placing related words in a circle labeled with the topic. I model this for younger students.

Non-negotiables:

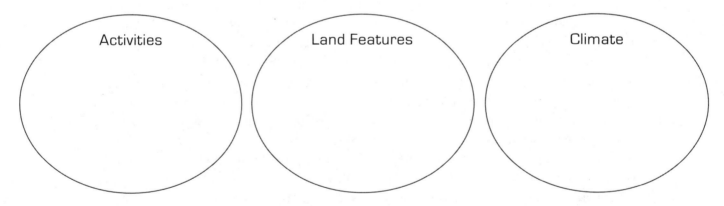

In their groups, students collect words for each of letter of the alphabet. Then they choose one word for each letter that they will explain, define, or describe in detail, being sure to address all the required topics. Here's what a group working on Iqaluit came up with;

Lessons for Guided Writing: Nonfiction © 2011 by Mary Sullivan, Scholastic Teaching Resources

notice that some letters only have one word, but other have several from which students will choose.

Iqaluit ABCs

A airport/Arctic/Arctic char/ aurora borealis

B Bay of Koojesse Inlet

C caribou

D dogsled/drumming/dancing

E early days

F frozen/fishing

G ground/games

H hunt/harbor/harpoons

I Inuit/inukshuk/iglu

J jobs

K kayaking

L lion seal/long winters

M midnight sun

N northern lights/Nunavut

O ocean

P polar bears

Q qimmig

R river

S sleds/snowmobiles/seals

T tundra

U ulu

V very isolated/very cold

W winter/walrus

eXtremely cold

Y Yellow airport

Z zero

A wonderful benefit of the alphabet book format is that is has built-in differentiation. Struggling writers will choose simpler words and phrases or create briefer and less complex explanations and definitions than stronger writers will. Students who excel in artistic ability will do the artwork with care and creativity that surpasses that of other students. (One pair of sixth graders chose to create rhyming couplets for all their facts!)

Focused Instruction

Once students have created the text for their alphabet book, we talk about choices for the artwork. Students see that stick figures or symbols work as well as realistic drawings. A sled can be drawn, for example, without the dogs, or a dog in harness can be drawn without the sled. Icicles, a snowflake, or a thermometer can symbolize the winter landscape.

If students are creating a book collaboratively, you might ask them to consider how their ability to work together and/or to meet timelines can be included in the rubric. If there is a technology component, you might discuss how this should be reflected in the assessment.

Creating a Rubric: Possible Elements for Alphabet Books

- All categories of non-negotiable content are covered

- Important aspects of the content and new knowledge are presented

- Facts are accurately presented

- Spelling, punctuation, and grammar are accurate
- Every letter has an entry relevant to the topic
- Vocabulary is precise and interesting
- Entries are unique and imaginative
- Graphics are instructive
- Graphics are interesting/attractive
- The overall presentation is neat and clean

TECH TIP

Students could be given the option of using clip art or graphics to illustrate their pages. If certain images are being repeated throughout the book, cutting and pasting can speed up the process significantly. In Microsoft Word, click on "Insert," then "Clip Art," and then click on "Clip Art" on Office Online to access thousands of items. (I remind students of the importance of correctly citing these digital sources.) Alternatively, students could use their digital cameras to shoot suitable photos for illustrations. Finding and creating these digital images is an interesting exercise in itself! I have had students create scenes and characters using Legos, Barbies, and their own costumes and makeup. For best results, give students the option to choose between hand-drawn work, clip art, images, or their own photos.

Independent Work

I often give students an opportunity to work on one book in pairs or groups of three. Students can post a sheet asking for suggestions for letters they are having difficulty with. We brainstorm together words that stand for difficult letters. Some of these words are new to students, and these become part of the word horde they use to get out of a tight spot on their project! For the letter Q in an animal book, the text might be (or begin with):

- *Quills: A porcupine has many sharp quills that help protect it from its enemies.*
- *Quite a bit of the mother fox's time is spent hunting for food for the kits.*
- *Quiet evenings are the best time to hear the loon's call on the lake.*
- *Quickly the deer vanish into the trees when they are disturbed during feeding.*

For Z we talk about how we might use words like *zany, zealous, zest, zigzag, zip, zippy, zillions, zero, zones,* and *zzzzz* (as in, *Zzzzz . . . daytime finds the bats hanging from the eaves, folded in sleep*).

Scaffolding: A Shared Product

Sometimes I ask students to work together in small groups to create text for the book, and then to produce (independently) separate copies of the book with their own printing and artwork. Group work, especially at the lower grade levels, moves the process along more quickly and allows all students the opportunity to participate in a successful product since there is a variety of roles and responsibilities involved. This is one way of training students in the techniques and strategies of writing in the genre while ensuring that every student experiences success. Students learn how to record sources they use, in case these are needed to clarify some information, as well as to name the sources they use in their books.

Independent Work

After doing one book together as a class (or several pages of one book with older students), students are much more confident about getting started on their own projects. Seeing what their peers have done also raises the bar for some students and pushes them to be more creative.

When students begin an independent project, we discuss all the information they are

TECH TIP

Using word processing software such as Microsoft Word can add polish to the finished alphabet book and let you include some special effects. In many of the published sample books, students will notice that the alphabet letters will be of different sizes and fonts, which draws the reader's attention. I am reminded of the illuminated manuscripts hand-drawn by monks during the Middle Ages, with their elaborate versals (the enlarged first letter of a word marking the beginning of text).

It is quick and easy to select the alphabet letter, change it to a more creative font, outline it, italicize it, and so on. I find it works best to model several fonts for the group and then discuss criteria for selection. We notice that some fonts may look cool but are difficult to read. This is a great opportunity to reflect on the intended audience and how it influences the final choice. Sometimes certain fonts suggest the item itself—for example, a spiky Q would be a great choice for *Quills*!

Students may decide to use a different font for each page, or choose one throughout the book for continuity, or even combine both options. If students have given their choice and can defend their selection, they are likely to be even more engaged and feel greater ownership of the final product.

TECH TIP

One alternative to creating a paper book is a multimedia presentation using programs such as PowerPoint or Notebook. It's simple to make a slide/page for each letter consisting of the letter, text, and an illustration, which is an excellent vehicle for learning a multimedia package. In addition to covering the curriculum content, students can now be learning specific software skills and effective presentation skills. See the Sample Teaching Sequence: Using Presentation Tools on the CD.

required to present. We clearly specify the expectations in a rubric or with focus questions to ensure that students know what content must be included. Even if students are all researching a different explorer, author, famous person, or geographic area, each report must include the same types of information.

Alphabet Books as a Language Arts Project

If the alphabet book is strictly a language arts project, it can take any number of forms: it can be autobiography or be based on video games, sports, animals, music, or any number of topics. These subjects have some very specialized terminology—students have certainly enhanced my own literacy on these topics over the years!

In my class we have a reverse dictionary, which lists words under subjects and categories. Most students have not encountered a reverse dictionary before. It's an excellent source of ideas for specific categories like musical instruments or boats and sailing terms (of which there were more than one hundred entries). Looking at the reverse dictionary has also inspired many students to choose certain subjects that matched up with their interests. Curious students dug up several hundred terms associated with horses, for example, listed under *horse, harness, horse racing,* and *saddle.* Under animal terms we found group names that surprised and entertained us: a *shrewdness* of apes, a *glaring* of cats, an *army* of frogs, and a *labor* of moles! Creating the alphabet books extended students' vocabularies—in areas of interest to them—in meaningful ways. Once students have learned to navigate in this genre with confidence, they may choose it for sharing information on future occasions when they are given a choice of format.

Porcupine Alphabet

A   *Alone is how you often find a porcupine.*

B   *Barbs on the ends of quills help them lodge in flesh.*

C   *Cousin rodents include the mouse, rat, woodchuck, squirrel, gopher, and beaver.*

D   *Dens are constructed in spring by female porcupines using shrubs, hollow logs, or spaces between rocks.*

E   *Erethizon dorsatum, the porcupine's scientific name, means "irritable back."*

F   *Front teeth of porcupines never stop growing.*

G   *Gnawing on tree branches and bark for food gives porcupines the odor of sawdust.*

H   *Hedgehogs are not related to porcupines even though they also have quills.*

I   *In the daytime the porcupine sleeps high up in the branches of a tree.*

J   *Just wake up and have your bed for breakfast if you are a porcupine.*

K   *Knobby rough skin on the bottom of the porcupine's feet helps it grip the tree as it climbs.*

L   *Life span of a porcupine is about nine years.*

M   *Mating porcupines dance together on their hind legs.*

N   *Nocturnal is the word we use for animals active at night. The porcupine is nocturnal.*

O   *Over 30,000 quills make up the porcupine's protective coat.*

P   *Porcupette is a young porcupine.*

Q   *Quills, or sharp spines, protect the porcupine from predators.*

R   *Rodent is the class of animal that has teeth for gnawing. Porcupines are rodents.*

S   *Singing a love song of hums, whistles, and grunts, the male travels the woods in search of a mate.*

T   *Trees offer porcupines safety, food, and a place to sleep.*

U   *Under the fur is a thick inner layer of hair grown in winter to keep the porcupine warm.*

V   *Very nearsighted, the porcupine relies on its sensitive nose to locate food and avoid danger.*

W   *Winter doesn't slow the porcupine down. He is active all year round.*

X   *eXtraordinary love of salt leads porcupines to munch on things with human perspiration on them.*

Y   *Young porcupines weigh about 1 pound when born. Their quills harden within a few hours.*

Z   *Zany orange teeth give the porcupine a bright smile!*

Graham, the maker of this porcupine alphabet, is a sixth-grade student whose sole source was a book from an excellent old Grolier series titled Getting to Know Nature's Children. *You will note that although this is a book for young people, some of the information Graham found in it was new to him, to his peers, and to me.*

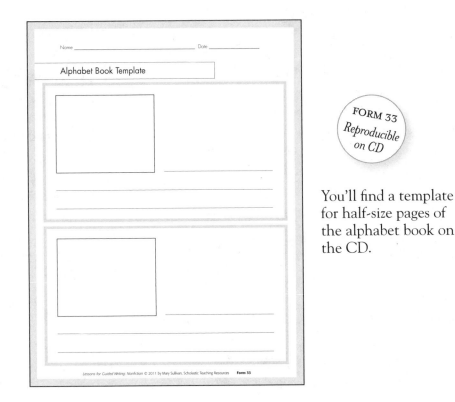

Name _____ Date _____

| Alphabet Book Template |

Lessons for Guided Writing: Nonfiction © 2011 by Mary Sullivan, Scholastic Teaching Resources   **Form 33**

FORM 33
Reproducible on CD

You'll find a template for half-size pages of the alphabet book on the CD.

Sharing Information Through the Strip Story

The strip story is a useful format for sharing information that students might gather for book reports, biographies, Greek myths, or reports on the travels of explorers. The strip story presentation requires students to prioritize information. It supports the learning of skills for identifying main ideas and details, as well as summarizing, and also enables students to demonstrate and develop artistic talent.

In a strip story, students create a story using a series of boxes, as in a cartoon strip. I usually use strips with ten to 12 boxes. Since students will need to know how many boxes they have to fill, make sure to decide on the number ahead of time.

Focused Instruction

Being able to show students samples is important. In the years before I had enough examples of the work of previous students, I made a quick mock-up of a few boxes just to give kids an idea of what we'd be making. We analyze the samples and discuss how to sequence and present information. Then we generate a rubric for the assignment.

Creating a Rubric: Possible Elements for Strip Stories

- All categories of non-negotiable content are covered
- Important aspects of the content and new knowledge are presented

Lessons for Guided Writing: Nonfiction © 2011 by Mary Sullivan, Scholastic Teaching Resources

- Facts are accurately presented
- Spelling, punctuation, and grammar in captions are accurate
- Vocabulary is precise and interesting
- Graphics are instructive (provide information in addition to what the captions tell us)
- Graphics are attractive/unique/imaginative
- The overall presentation is neat and clean

Independent Work

The process of gathering data is the same as for any other research project that demands specific content and utilizes focus questions. Students do research using various sources and turn their findings into notes and/or fact cards. Having separate cards is especially useful because students can move them around and put them in a sensible order as an organizational activity.

From their research notes and/or fact cards, students create the text for the boxes of the strip story.

Scaffolding

Once students have completed their text sequence, they meet with peers to go through the checklist of information required based on the focus questions. This provides them with an opportunity to catch missing elements before they hand work in. Students hand in the text information for the boxes, numbered from 1 to 10, before they draw any pictures.

Feedback

Once students have an approved sequence, I edit their ten text pieces (statements or paragraphs, depending on grade level) for conventions, so the drawings won't have to be redone because of errors in the text.

Sharing Information Through Posters

I consider posters a great nonfiction genre because they invite so much audience interest in the information they present. Teachers who use bulletin boards to display student work know that middle school students respond to these displays every bit as enthusiastically as elementary students. Posters are inviting because of the wonderful artwork students do, and they also allow us to increase the size of print so that the accompanying text can be read from the wall.

Focused Instruction

I ask students to imagine how much of the information they gather in a research project they might be able to depict without words or with very few words. Before we undertake the poster assignment, I gather pieces of graphic information to show students the many kinds of information that can be shared in visually. Most social studies and science texts will give you a broad array of examples—graphs, drawings, symbols, icons, and maps.

With older students it is interesting to send them on a textbook scavenger hunt (for homework or in class) to locate samples of the kinds of information that can be shared either without words or with very few words. Parents often join the project.

The lessons for working on a poster assignment will depend on the particular area of research or study, and the preliminary steps will mirror those for other genres. Setting focus questions and limiting the number of words the poster can have force students to reshape information from the source texts they have consulted. This is a good follow-up project to summarizing practice. For the graphic component I allow students to draw, use photographs or symbols, or make a collage to appeal to viewers and contribute to the poster's subject.

My fifth and sixth graders created posters to share information about animals. Students

---

A Note About the Artwork

The strip stories make attractive displays and allow students to view, in an accessible format, information from curriculum content areas.

Students should be encouraged to draw symbols or stick people if they are intimidated by the art aspect of the project. For artistic students it is important to have opportunities where, because of their particular talent, they shine. These students sometimes experience less success and confidence with written work. In real life, many people make their living using their artistic abilities, and teachers who make these skills part of classroom work rightly imply that these abilities are valuable and important.

received extra marks for every piece of information they expressed graphically. Some students were very inventive; one drew a tiny map of the province and shaded the areas where the animal in question was found. Since students are also viewing and collecting information from graphs and symbols, I think it helps them to notice, interpret, and use such visual representations if they are employing them in their own efforts to share information.

Feedback

I created a reflection sheet to help students critically examine their developing posters, first independently and then in discussion with peers. They may decide to make final additions or revisions to the piece, or the sheet may simply provide a means for students to think critically about the poster before handing it in for my evaluation. In this case, students hand the reflection in with the poster. (This activity with

| Name _____ | Date _____ |

Poster Project Evaluation

Presenter's Name: _____ Date: _____

Evaluator's Name: _____ Activity: _____

Assign a mark from 1 to 3 (3 being the highest ranking).

	1	2	3
The message/information about the subject is presented fully and clearly.	1	2	3
The material is presented in an interesting way.	1	2	3
The purpose of the presentation is evident.	1	2	3
The presentation of the poster showed skill in the use of this medium.	1	2	3
The poster was neat and polished in its presentation.	1	2	3

The thing I liked best about the poster was _____
_____
_____

One suggestion I would make is _____
_____
_____

Lessons for Guided Writing: Nonfiction © 2011 by Mary Sullivan, Scholastic Teaching Resources   For

FORM 34
Reproducible on CD

TECH TIP

Again, there are a number of electronic versions of the poster project. Many students are experienced with using digital photo programs that allow them to transform the pictures and add text and sound. Photoshop Elements is one program. There are online versions as well. One popular site is Piknic. Many students accustomed to working with social networking sites like Facebook will be skilled in adapting images for their profile pictures.

EduGlogster is a Web site where students can create remarkable posters with graphics, fonts, videos, and special effects. Gone are the large sheets of poster board with a few small graphics, some text, and a large title at the top. Instead, students can insert and manipulate endless images and text. Rather than erasing and redoing, one click lets them change and rearrange. A large gallery of completed posters can provide inspiration as well.

questions modified to fit a particular topic would be useful with other projects. You might also use the reflection sheet to create an evaluation rubric with your students.)

When I want students to practice peer assessment (and/or self-assessment), in which they apply a numerical evaluation to their work, I use a simple form like the one on page 129.

Sharing Information Through Letters

When students transpose information from found sources to a letter format, they are forced to disengage from the source text, extract the information they need, and utilize this information in a new format. Regardless of the type of content you study with your students, exposing them to authentic letters from different periods of history is a valuable way to begin a discussion about the unique characteristics of letters as literary forms. Students can examine samples of such letters as a class or in small groups and discuss and analyze their distinct characteristics.

Critical Literacy and Letters

This is also an excellent opportunity to discuss the whole concept of differing perspectives. A French settler's perspective on the French-English battles in early Canadian history would certainly differ from an Englishman's. The first-nations people had a different sense of what was agreed upon in the treaties than did the white men who framed them. Students can experiment with writing letters from various perspectives about a topic as they take on a certain persona in their letters.

Focused Instruction: Analysis

In small groups, have students examine samples of letters from their social studies textbooks or from the Internet. As they analyze the letters, they might use a form similar to the one here to guide their discussion.

This analysis and discussion gets students thinking about the research they will be doing

Name _____ Date _____

| Analysis of a Historical Letter |

Directions: Answer the following questions to analyze the characteristics of a historical letter.

1. What do we know about this person from what he or she tells us in the letter?

2. What further information and impressions can we gain from the tone and style of the letter?

3. Who is the letter's intended recipient?

4. What seems to be the purpose of the letter?

5. What can we infer about the relationship between the correspondents?

6. What actual information does the letter contain?

FORM 35
Reproducible on CD

Lessons for Guided Writing: Nonfiction © 2011 by Mary Sullivan, Scholastic Teaching Resources

Lessons for Guided Writing: Nonfiction © 2011 by Mary Sullivan, Scholastic Teaching Resources

into the characteristics and circumstances of their fictional/historical letter-writer, in order to share factual information about a time or an event through the letters they will write.

Sample Assignment: Letters From the Colony

Focused Instruction: Collecting and Generating Material

In this sample lesson, students are studying the establishment of the Canadian colonies. Students must select a colonist to research and then write a letter in the voice of that person to share what they've learned about the person and the times he or she lived in. Some students will choose to compose a letter from one of women known as the king's daughters to a friend or relative in France. Students will need to create the character. *What is her background? Is she excited about this opportunity for adventure, or is she fearful and bitter that this is her only option? What is her new life like? What does she miss about her old life?* Besides creating the character, students will need to research details about daily life in the New World.

Scaffolding Through Collaboration

As the research is progressing, students who are writing about a similar group of individuals, such as merchants or aristocrats, can meet in their respective groups and share discussion and information about the backgrounds of their common subjects, their subjects' New World prospects and circumstances, and the hopes and fears these individuals might have had. This expert group discussion will assist students who might be at a loss sorting through the text on their own.

Focused Instruction: Identifying Criteria

Before the letter-writing, you and your students need to decide on the criteria for evaluation, keeping some of the following factors in mind.

Creating a Rubric: Possible Elements for Historical Letters

- The letter's purpose is clear to the reader.

- The letter is interesting and shows that the writer is knowledgeable about the background and circumstances of the fictional character (the *content* requirements).

- The letter shows that the student has researched aspects of the daily life and the prospects of the character.

- The voice behind the fictional writer seems believable.

- The mechanics of the writing show control of the conventions of spelling, punctuation, and grammar.

Research-based letters can cover almost any aspect of curriculum. A letter can be composed from the point of view of a polar explorer who is dying, a visitor to Peru writing about historic Inca sites, a honeybee describing the building and functioning of the hive, a citizen protesting the nuclear testing undertaken by the government, a resident (of any state or country being studied) extolling the beauty and opportunities of "home" to a prospective visitor, a famous scientist, an athlete, or a homeless person. Information can be shared in letters about almost any person, event, place, or time being studied. This genre in particular allows students to attend to the concepts of persona and audience, because unlike other genres, the letter has a strong focus on the roles of sender and receiver.

TECH TIP

In another version of this assignment, students can use the social networking that they are so familiar and comfortable with (texting, Facebook, tweeting, and so on) to create a conversation based on curriculum. For example, what description of himself would a samurai soldier post on his Facebook wall? Who would be his friends? What sorts of messages would they leave for him, and what would an ongoing conversation look like?

Since a tweet can only consist of 140 characters, students have to be able to synthesize their research and information on a topic into succinct messages. This format works well for describing a particular event in history.

Lessons for Guided Writing: Nonfiction © 2011 by Mary Sullivan, Scholastic Teaching Resources

Like personal letters, news articles can be used to share research findings in social studies, science, and other subjects. Students will have to transpose and reshape the material they have gathered from text sources, which forces them to more closely examine the information and discourages copying. Because students have already studied and practiced writing news pieces, they can now concentrate on the content for the article. Consider your curricular objectives for the assignment, and then create a list of criteria that must be addressed in the piece and work to create a rubric that clearly shows the target. (The newspaper rubric created earlier can be modified for this assignment; simply add the content criteria, such as including particular factual information, using correct data, and so on.)

Scaffolding: Structured Collaboration

For this assignment, students might imagine a historical event, discovery, or exploration being reported as a news story in the time period when it occurred. To write the news item, students would take what they know about writing a news article and apply that to the area they researched.

Because students have already written one or more news articles and understand the criteria for evaluating them, they can bring their first drafts to a peer-editing group for some initial feedback on the lead, the tone, the language, or the slant of the article (see pages 52–58 for lessons on these topics). I have the groups deal with one focus at a time, reminding them in advance exactly what we are looking for in the draft.

Peer Editing: The Newspaper Article

1. Look for the answers to the 4 W's: Who, What, Where, and When in the first two to three sentences.
2. Suggest ways in which the writer can condense the beginning to form the lead.
3. Look for colloquial or informal vocabulary and suggest alternatives (see chart on page 56 for suggestions).
4. Check that the verbs are in the past tense throughout.
5. Ask the writer whether he or she knows the source of the facts in his article (original text source).
6. Decide whether the body of the article could be beefed up or whether it seems

---

Name _____ Date _____

Peer Editing: The Newspaper Article

Directions: Respond to the following prompts to help the writer revise his or her newspaper article.

1. Are the 4 W's—Who, What, Where, and When—in the first two to three sentences?

2. Suggest ways in which the writer can condense the beginning to form the lead.

3. Look for colloquial or informal vocabulary and suggest alternatives.

4. Check that the verbs are in the past tense throughout.

5. Ask the writer whether he or she knows the source of the facts in his or her article.

6. Decide whether the rest of the article following the lead could be beefed up or whether it seems satisfactory as it is. Is any additional information needed? Would quotations from people who were involved be helpful?

7. When you have read the whole article, reflect upon whether the headline is effective and fitting for the article's content and slant.

8. Check for spelling, punctuation, and grammatical correctness.

Lessons for Guided Writing: Nonfiction © 2011 by Mary Sullivan, Scholastic Teaching Resources   Fo

FORM 36
Reproducible on CD

Of course, word processing creates a professional-looking final article, simply by using columns in Word, inserting a graphic, and wrapping text around it. For students ready for a little more, Microsoft Publisher (standard with Microsoft Office) comes with premade templates. I find that in every group of students, there are always a few who are technology whizzes. I hire them as publishers. When students finish typing their pieces, they pass them on to the publishers, who turn the entire group's work into a polished publication. After this initial newspaper, the first publishers are then able to train a few more students, and soon we have a room full of experts!

The Tools menu in Word also gives you the option of calculating a readability score. Most newspapers are written at a sixth-grade reading level. A great exercise is to have students calculate the readability score on a beginning draft of their article. Once they have edited the piece and made more sophisticated word choices, the students can again check the readability score. Seeing the difference before and after an editing session can be a very motivating way to get writers to focus on their word choices.

satisfactory as it is. Is any additional information needed? Would quotations from people who were involved be helpful?

7. When you have read the whole article, reflect upon whether the headline is effective and fitting for the article's content and slant.

8. Check for spelling, punctuation, and grammatical correctness.

The Report: A Formal Presentation of Factual Information From Student Research

This genre tends to be a vehicle for sharing researched material in the content areas of social studies, science, and health. As a language arts teacher I use this format quite rarely. As I mentioned in the introduction, I prefer using letters, news articles, alphabet books, posters, strip stories, and oral presentations in order to sidestep the dreaded issue of students copying from text sources. However, the report has its place. Depending upon what it is exactly that we want students to learn, we can set out the field of exploration and the kinds of material we want them to search for and collect.

I like kids to tackle a common assignment with shared focus questions so I can teach them how to do research and present the information. At the same time, I open up the sources students can use to allow readers of differing abilities to handle the assignment. In the Famous People assignment that follows, for example, I have had students use everything from picture books to thick biographies and Internet sites as source material.

Focused Instruction: The Report

Since it is always critical for students to understand the purpose of embarking on new learning, it's important to share examples of reports that exemplify the end product you have in mind. Many current literacy programs utilize reports as nonfiction components as well as social studies and science materials. Educational magazines such as *Cobblestone* and *Cricket* contain sample reports on topics ranging from Mesopotamia to music, the Silk Road to spiders. (Of course, magazine articles come in a range of other formats, including interviews, reviews, columns, and other types of writing.)

Select one or more reports that have all the components you will include in the current assignment and share these with students. Point out how various aspects of the report's layout present information and perspectives, as do elements like sidebars, graphics, and pictures surrounding the actual text components. With the technology tools that Kelli's students use, kids get very interested in presenting information through graphs, maps, and cartoons. They love using fonts and colors to add visual interest to their reports.

Showing students the effectiveness of these elements *before* they begin to work on the report heightens their motivation and sparks their imagination about what is possible. It's good for students to have some incubation time, as well as some room for exploration in the beginning phase of the writing.

I stress with students the importance of thoughtful information-gathering and the fact that all the components need to serve the main purpose of the report. For example, you might point out that as part of a report about the Yukon Quest dogsled race, a picture of husky puppies is less relevant (no matter how cute they are) than a picture of the winning team or musher. Students see that reports are divided into distinct sections separated by spaces and subtitles. This might be a time to point out that these headings function much the way transition words and phrases do in linking the paragraphs in an essay.

Assignment: A Biographical Report

In designing the lessons that support this writing assignment, I want to choose a topic for the entire class so that I can provide instruction to all of my students at once. I also want that topic to be open-ended enough that it allows students to research and write about something that holds genuine interest for them. The topic needs to be one for which there will be accessible information for all students. A topic that fits these requirements, one that I have used at every grade level, is biography.

The availability of texts across many reading levels also supports differentiation within a common assignment. When I assigned this topic to fifth graders, I had the entire range of abilities, from a student who couldn't decide between researching Benjamin Franklin and Leonardo Da Vinci to one who used a picture book to do her research on Charles Goodyear. David read both thick books and then chose to write about Ben Franklin. Tracy discovered fascinating facts about Goodyear from her picture book, including that his wife had him put in jail for the offensive-smelling experiments he carried out in the kitchen!

Focused Instruction

Students use the biography they've chosen as their first source of material. Students who cannot find all the information they need in their biography can do further research on the Internet. The same kinds of preliminary activities discussed in Chapter 5 can be used with this research. We talk about what will be important to note and record as we read. Together we make a list of the kinds of information we will attempt to gather. Our list includes the following:

Famous People: Guide to Making Notes

- Where and when did the person live?
- What was it like in that time and place?
- What do you know about the person's early life?
- Who were some of the important people in the person's life? How or why were they important?
- What was the earliest sign of this person's interest in the area for which he or she is famous?
- What did he or she do to pursue or learn more about the area of interest?
- What was his or her first success?
- What were his or her later accomplishments?

Name _____ Date _____

Famous People: Guide to Making Notes

Name of Person: _____

1. Where and when did the person live?

2. What was it like in that time and place?

3. What do you know about the person's early life?

4. Who were some of the people important in the person's life? Why were they important?

5. What was the earliest sign of this person's interest in the area for which he or she is famous?

6. What did he or she do to pursue or learn more about the area of interest?

7. What was his or her first success?

8. What were his or her later accomplishments?

9. How did this person's life end?

10. What is important to us today about the person's accomplishment(s)?

FORM 37
Reproducible on CD

Lessons for Guided Writing: Nonfiction © 2011 by Mary Sullivan, Scholastic Teaching Resources   **Form**

Lessons for Guided Writing: Nonfiction © 2011 by Mary Sullivan, Scholastic Teaching Resources

- How did this person's life end?
- What is important to us today about the person's accomplishment(s)?

Scaffolding

I give students sticky notes to place on the pages of their biography where they find the answers to their focus questions. This allows them to come back and make notes. I also supply students with a copy of the questions to guide their note-taking. This list spells out the non-negotiable aspects of the fact finding. As students locate the various required information, they jot notes onto a graphic organizer consisting of empty boxes labeled to match the list. These brief notes disengage them from the wording found in the text.

> *It's interesting that as teachers we often think that the very capable and talented students need different (harder or more) questions or assignments than the rest of the class. I have found that if the assignment is open-ended (if students are allowed to choose their biographical subject, in this example) and the questions ask for critical thinking (interpretation, analysis, comparison, hypothesis, and so on) the giftedness shows in the response. An assignment like this will result in responses that demonstrate a wide range of skill and sophistication.*

Focused Instruction

Now students and I are ready to look at the components of the report as they will appear in the finished version. I have decided that the report will be comprised of these eight elements:

Components of the Report

1. A title (see A Word About Titles on page 87)
2. An introductory section, which tells who the subject is and when and where he or she lived
3. A "claim to fame" section telling what made the person famous
4. A development section that details influences on the person, early accomplishments, and travel or study
5. A concluding section that deals with the importance/implications of the person's contribution
6. A "word from the writer" section in which the writer tells how studying this person has affected him or her
7. A sidebar that tells some little-known fact or surprising or interesting detail
8. Graphics and/or pictures that add interest and/or information to the report

Assessment

This activity leads naturally to the creation of a scoring rubric that includes these components and any other expectations regarding content and form. Some of the criteria to do with factual accuracy, vocabulary, and conventions will be similar to (or modifications of) criteria for other writing assignments. If some particular aspect of technology has been incorporated, this should also be reflected in the rubric.

Creating a Rubric: Possible Elements for Reports

- Title is interesting/relevant
- The report contains all sections listed on the Components of the Report form
- Each section contains the required information
- Facts are accurately reported
- Graphics and/or pictures add interest and information
- Overall presentation is attractive, clean, and neat
- Writing is in the student's own words
- Writing is error-free
- Vocabulary is precise and descriptive
- Sentence structure is varied

As students gain experience with the report format and the technology tools, they can be given more choices about the format of the report. In the beginning I want students to know

This assignment would work well as a multimedia project using PowerPoint, Notebook, or other presentation software. I prefer to have students work with partners when creating these presentations because these programs entail a fair amount of problem-solving. (See appendix on teaching kids to use presentation software.) If students create the presentation together, they can each work on different topics. I've used a side-by-side format successfully—for example, a page on the important accomplishments of the individual would have Thomas Edison on one side and Leonardo Da Vinci on the other. Having a partner gives each child support, not only with the technical aspects of creating the presentation but also with processing the information.

exactly what they are aiming for, and I want the assignment to be contained enough so they will not be overwhelmed.

Scaffolding

Students now meet in partners or small groups to share information from their completed Guide to Making Notes. Students discuss which pieces of information should be used in the various text sections of their report. A visual organizer with spaces for these text sections might be helpful for students at some grade levels. Alternately, simply numbering facts in their notes can help them to chunk information as preparation for writing the various sections. Completing the final section (A Word From the Writer) will help struggling writers and verbal processors to articulate their thoughts about what they learned or how they were influenced by the famous person they investigated.

Practice

Drawing from a list of requirements or a graphic organizer, students write a draft of their composition.

Feedback

Your response to the draft provides students with the direction they need to sharpen the organization and coherence of the composition. Editing of the conventions prepares students to make such corrections on a final draft.

Writers need varying degrees of feedback on the draft they hand in, depending on whether the finished product is to be shared beyond the classroom. Not every composition needs to be worked on until it is error-free. As long as writers see the errors they have made, they learn from them.

Conclusion

Kelli and I set out to share some strategies around the teaching of nonfiction writing. We told our editor that the result would be a slim book. It turned out otherwise! Once we got started, the manuscript ran away with us. Even though I began by suggesting that we need to recognize and legitimize the many, many forms of nonfiction writing besides research essays and reports, I hadn't fully recognized them myself until I reflected on all the kinds of writing (which were indeed nonfiction formats) that I have done with my students over the years.

As each type of nonfiction writing presented itself to me, I had to acknowledge the importance to different students of various kinds of writing. The student who shone in the autobiography was not as strong on the report writing, and the student who needed instruction and support to make notes and record information loved the poster assignment. I reflected as I went along how each of the many formats have taught me something about writing, or have been useful and important in some practical way over the years to me as a teacher and as a writer.

The lessons, as they are presented in this book, cannot be taught in a single year, especially with the technology component as rich and thorough as it is! I simply didn't want to delete from the manuscript something that might be important or useful to some teacher at some grade level . . . to some student who perhaps missed this strategy, or that technique or opportunity . . . and has now come to your class. Forgive me the indulgence here. The text will take you beyond one grade level, and beyond one year. You are, in any case, meant to pick and choose from among the suggestions here according to the mandates of your particular curricula, according to your own personal teaching agenda, and your pedagogical wisdom.

It is my hope, and Kelli's as well, that you have found here useful tools and nourishment to share in the writing communities you will establish this year and in the future!

—**Mary Sullivan**

Appendix

The following Web sites are mentioned throughout the book but are gathered together here with a brief description for easy access. The list is also found on the accompanying CD.

Graphic Organizers

Inspiration: http://www.inspiration.com/ A free 30-day trial is available as well as Kidspiration, a version intended for students from K–5. Check out the video demo.

SMART Ideas: http://smarttech.com/smartideas SMART Technologies concept-mapping software designed for use with the SMART interactive whiteboard.

Gliffy: http://www.gliffy.com

Online diagram software with a free version available

MindMeister: http://www.mindmeister.com/ Online mind mapping that allows for collaborative use. A free version is available.

Collaborative Writing

PrimaryPad: http://primarypad.com A collaborative online word processor designed with schools in mind. Extremely easy to use, no sign-up required, and great for sharing with everyone!

Wallwisher: http://www.wallwisher.com/ An online bulletin board that lets users put up multiple sticky notes.

Google Docs: http://docs.google.com Everyone's favorite site, Google, has a wide variety of applications to choose from. This one allows a user to create a document, and for other users to add, comment, and make changes while online. Requires all users to have a Google account.

Videoconferencing

Google Talk: www.google.com/talk/ A free application that allows text, voice, and video chat between users.

Other Useful Sites

Skype: www.skype.com Allows voice and video calls to other Skype users. Check out the video demo.

Multimedia

VoiceThread: www.voicethread.com An online application that lets you post images, videos, and documents, and have users comment on your projects through text, audio, and video. Easy to use and highly engaging for students.

Comic Life: http://www.comiclife.com/ Quickly and easily create comics, photo albums, and more. A great way for students to illustrate research.

Picknik: http://www.picnik.com/ Free, easy to use online photo editing.

Glogster: http://www.glogster.com/ Free, easy to use online application for creating interactive posters. Use text, music, images, and video to create a unique presentation.

Movie Maker: http://download.live.com/moviemaker Create movies and slide shows using photos, videos, and music. Free download for Windows users.

Photo Story 3: http://www.microsoft.com/windowsxp/using/digitalphotography/photostory/default.mspx Create slide shows with photos, music, and special effects. Free download for Windows users.

Newspapers

Onlinenewspapers.com: http://www.onlinenewspapers.com/ Links to thousands of newspapers from around the world, collected in one easily accessible place.

Paperboy: http://www.thepaperboy.com/ Links to newspapers around the world, as well as today's headlines and a rotating gallery of front pages.

Archives

Archives Canada: http://www. archivescanada.ca/ A gateway to more than 800 sites across Canada, organized and linked for easy use. Also has a list of international archival resources.

Archives in the Classroom: http://www.ataoc.ca/archives/main.html An interactive virtual train station that enables users to learn about the lives of Canadian immigrants through photos, documents, and other personal evidence. The censored prisoner-of-war postcards carry a heavy emotional impact.

I Remain—A Digital Archive of Letters, Manuscripts, and Ephemera: http://digital.lib.lehigh.edu/remain/index.html Lehigh University's Special Collections department's autographed letters and correspondence. Organized by daily life, arts, features, honor, language, history, science, travel, war and politics, working writer and writing through the centuries, these documents offer a fascinating glimpse of what life was like for both celebrities and ordinary folk.

Virtual Reference Library: http://www.virtualreferencelibrary.ca/ Use the Digital Collections tab to uncover pieces of Canadian history.

Digital Images

Pics4Learning.com: http://pics4learning.com Thousands of images gathered together in one site for educators and students.

Wikimedia Commons: http://commons.wikimedia.org Millions of images, sound, and video clips available for free. Usage must follow the terms specified by the author.

MorgueFile: http://www.morguefile.com/ A large assortment of free images available for all users of the Web.

Stock.xchang: http://www.sxc.hu Another free photo site with thousands of images.

Blogs

Edublogs: http://www.edublogs.org An easy to use site providing lots of information, assistance and advice about blogging. Free versions are available.

Surveys

Zoomerang: http://www.zoomerang.com Easy to create online surveys. Free version is available.

SurveyMonkey: http://www.surveymonkey.com Create free online surveys and questionnaires quickly.

Other Useful Web sites

SMART Notebook Express: http://express.smarttech.com This site lets you view, work with, and save Notebook files online. Great for sharing Notebook projects students have completed at school with friends and family.

TinyURL: http://tiny.cc/ Lets you take a long Web address and shorten it to one that is easier to use.

2Learn's Top Level Domains and Country Codes: http://www.netknowhow.ca/nkhSRcc.html A description of domain meaning and country codes, useful for helping students recognize bias on Web sites.

Snopes: http://www.snopes.com A fact-checking Web site and valuable tool for anyone who's ever wondered about the authenticity of an e-mail or Web site.

2Learn.ca's Plagiarism Sleuth: http://www.netknowhow.ca/stringsearchnew.html Concerned about the veracity of a student's work? Use this helpful tool to find out! Step-by-step directions are provided.

Rubistar: http://rubistar.4teachers.org/ Choose from generic rubrics, or customize and create your own. Save your rubrics online, and access them from home or school.

Storybird: http://www.storybird.com It's a snap for users to create stories using few or many images at Storybird.

TodaysMeet: http://todaysmeet.com In every meeting, there are always side conversations. This site projects those questions, comments, and feedback for everyone to see, and provides immediate feedback on the presentation. Try it!

Reading Rants! Out of the Ordinary Teen Booklists!: http://www.readingrants.org A librarian-run interactive blog aimed at young adults. Lots of book lists and recommendations.

CD Contents

Sample Teaching Sequence: Using Graphic Organizers . . . . Using GO.pdf

Sample Teaching Sequence: Using Presentation Tools . . . . Using Tools.pdf

Appendix: List of Web Sites . . . . Appendix.pdf

Forms

Form Number	Form Name	Page Reference
Form 1	Creating a Rubric: Guided Questions	18
Form 2	Creating a Rubric: A Guide for Students	19
Form 3	Rubric Template (4x4)	19
Form 4	Rubric Template (4x5)	19
Form 5	Rough Notes for the Thanksgiving Letters	25
Form 6	Possible Introductions and Conclusions to the Thanksgiving Letter	27
Form 7	Letters of Commendation: Prompts for Generating Ideas	33
Form 8	Fan Letters	37
Form 9	Questions and Sentence Stems for Functional Letters	41
Form 10	Standardized Test Prep: Letter	45
Form 11	Analysis of the News Article	47
Form 12	Texts for Comparing Genres: Narrative, News Article, Essay	50
Form 13	Comparison of Three Genres Chart	51
Form 14	Newspaper Articles Written by Students	53
Form 15	Models of News Articles With Different Slants	54–55
Form 16	Notes for My News Article	59
Form 17	Chronology Frame	62–63
Form 18	Opposites Frame	63
Form 19	Categories Frame	64
Form 20	Concentric Circles Frame	65
Form 21	Spokes-in-a-Wheel Frame	65
Form 22	Autobiographical Timeline	70
Form 23	Response to Your Autobiographical Essay/Memoir	72
Form 24	Character Profile: Evidence From the Text	73
Form 25	Sample Literary Essay Introductions	77–78
Form 26	Analysis of the Persuasive Essay	80
Form 27	Material for My Soapbox Essay	83
Form 28	Guide to the Language of Fact and Opinion	99
Form 29	Note-Taking From a Video or Presentation	105
Form 30	Notes for a Field Trip	113
Form 31	Tips for Creating Interview Questions	115
Form 32	Tips for Conducting the Interview	116
Form 33	Alphabet Book Template	126
Form 34	Poster Project Evaluation	129
Form 35	Analysis of a Historical Letter	130
Form 36	Peer Editing: The Newspaper Article	133
Form 37	Famous People: Guide to Making Notes	136
Form 38	Guide to Lesson Design	

Lessons for Guided Writing: Nonfiction © 2011 by Mary Sullivan, Scholastic Teaching Resources